'Provocative and original.'

Gideon Rachman, Chief Foreign Affairs Correspondent,
Financial Times

'Endlessly inventive, restlessly cosmopolitan, Bruno Maçães has written an essential book with which to think about the Covid crisis and its implications for our future.'

Adam Tooze, historian and author of
Crashed: How A Decade of Financial Crises Changed The World

'With typical panache, Maçães sets out the story of what went wrong when Covid-19 spread around the world—and why. Gripping, terrifying and revealing in equal measures.'

Peter Frankopan, author of
The Silk Roads: A New History of the World

'An important book. Bruno Maçães once again asks the crucial questions.'

Ece Temelkuran, journalist, novelist, political commentator and author of *How to Lose a Country: The 7 Steps from Democracy to Dictatorship*

'2020 was the true start of the twenty-first century, marking the death of an old world, and a recognition that new ideas in culture, politics, science and technology have become possible. Maçães does an excellent job of taking us through some core themes of the world to come.'

Vitalik Buterin, founder of Ethereum and *Bitcoin Magazine*

GEOPOLITICS FOR THE END TIME

BRUNO MAÇÃES

Geopolitics for the End Time

From the Pandemic to the Climate Crisis

HURST & COMPANY, LONDON

First published in the United Kingdom in 2021 by
C. Hurst & Co. (Publishers) Ltd.,
83 Torbay Road, London, NW6 7DT
© Bruno Maçães, 2021
All rights reserved.

The right of Bruno Maçães to be identified as the author of
this publication is asserted by him in accordance with the
Copyright, Designs and Patents Act, 1988.

The quote from Norbert Wiener's *The Human Use of Human
Beings* (Garden City, NY: Doubleday, 1954) is reproduced
with the kind permission of Penguin Random House.

A Cataloguing-in-Publication data record for this book
is available from the British Library.

ISBN: 9781787385542

This book is printed using paper from registered sustainable
and managed sources.

Printed in Great Britain by Bell & Bain Ltd, Glasgow

www.hurstpublishers.com

Cover image: Ludwig Meidner, 'Apocalyptic City',
1913 © Ludwig Meidner-Archiv, Jüdisches Museum der Stadt
Frankfurt am Main

To the victims of the pandemic. May they be remembered.

May we have the courage to face the eventual doom of our civilization as we have the courage to face the certainty of our personal doom. The simple faith in progress is not a conviction belonging to strength, but one belonging to acquiescence and hence to weakness.

Norbert Wiener, *The Human Use of Human Beings* (1954)

Geopolitics

S	States
→	Globalization
☐	Nature

The diagram is meant as a summary of this book, and therefore as a summary in visual form of the geopolitical doctrine contained therein. The reader is encouraged to return to this page after reading the book. The diagram was minted as a non-fungible token, or NFT, and sold to an anonymous buyer in February 2021. It can be found on the Ethereum blockchain, block 11848744, where presumably it can survive the outcome of even a worldwide nuclear conflagration.

CONTENTS

CONTENTS

SPACESHIP EARTH

There is something about life during the pandemic that cannot but remind me of space travel. You wake up, walk around the spaceship, connect the video messaging, go back to sleep, knowing it is still nine or twelve months to planet Trantor or planet Terminus, or the next galaxy system, where we expect to arrive...

This was how it felt: leaving the world behind, retreating to some protected sphere where the whole point was to let time pass until it was once again safe to go out into the world, albeit a new or changed one. The first tragedy is that many never made it to the safety of this time machine. They were left behind and their deaths were especially grim because of the complete loneliness surrounding them. The numbers kept growing, but the numbers alone fail to explain how the pandemic became, for an age used to life, the purest representation of death. It was the deadly struggle in the emergency or high dependency units where the machines helping you breathe by forcing air into the lungs at high pressure made patients feel they were suffocating. It was the moment when they had to be intubated, knowing there was a one in two chance of never waking up again. It was the fear of becoming death not only for ourselves but for others as well. The fear of becoming the vehicle of their deaths and the fear of being left alone in our dying moments so that others might not die with us. Even when hospitals started to allow relatives to be present at the moment of death, they had to do so from a distance and while wearing full protective equipment. As one doctor put it in a moving testimonial written this year, all the Covid patients who die do so alone: "There is nobody to hold their hand. Nobody to comfort them. Nobody to tell them they love them."[1]

Even survival became a form of death. It was soon apparent that the best way to survive was to sacrifice a portion of our lives, to give up on a few months or a few years of the life we knew and loved in order to get the remainder back. It was this bargain that reminded me of space travel and the inconvenient fact that space travel, in books and movies, tends to be paid in life years, the time to make the journey from planet to planet, through dead sidereal space.

It was a common experience, bringing together most people around the world over the last two years. Some sacrificed their globe-trotting habits. Others postponed weddings or were forced to close down their small businesses. Children lost a year of school. Older people stopped meeting their grandchildren; many became victims of the pandemic before that cruel exclusion could be lifted. We stopped seeing our friends, or did so with so many rules and with so much caution that nothing felt the same. Jobs were lost and personal plans abandoned. We were all looking through glass. The largest and busiest cities in the world seemed entirely empty for long periods. Those photographs will probably endure for a century or longer as the main symbol of the pandemic. I remember reading one post on social media where a young woman asked if she could postpone entering her thirties for a year, given how the last year had been lost. It was a way to capture the experience for those who survived it. Our sense of grief now extends to all the time we are never getting back.

The experience reflects something both novel and important about our historical moment. This retreat from the world into a protected technological abode would not have been possible in the past. As we shall see later in this book, it was not possible a century ago during the great influenza pandemic known as the Spanish flu, when the tools we had available to manage our economies and societies were relatively primitive. Imagine closing all schools before a transition to remote learning became possible. "Try to imagine what 2020 would have been like without Google, Amazon, Zoom, Slack or any of the other online services." As Noah

Smith shows, it is a nightmarish vision. Everyone would have to use physical stores. "Imagine the lines stretching around the block as impatient mask-wearing crowds stood six feet apart, waiting hours for the chance to buy some toilet paper or soap." People would have to go into their offices or else firms would have to halt operations. This was the reality for many frontline workers, of course, but large parts of the economy found a much better solution and fared much better. Those economists who have argued that the value of digital technology has not shown up in economic growth figures were blinded by normal times. Sometimes technology works as an insurance policy and we have to measure its impact against the state of the world during an emergency.[2]

It is certainly possible that this great migration to remote life might not happen again in the future. Some have speculated that, assuming new breakthroughs in biomedicine take place in the near future, Covid could well turn out to be the last great pandemic. In 2020, caught by a dangerous environmental threat but capable of building an artificial environment protected from it, we simply retreated to our terrestrial spaceship.

For me the most vivid memories of the pandemic will probably remain those from the week in Istanbul during which the management of my hotel each day announced a new closure: first the pool and gym, then the restaurant, then the cafe. One morning my floor had become pitch dark. Soon the hotel itself announced it would close in two days, forcing us to move out. Then the shops closed and finally the parks. The airport stopped working.

As I write these lines, we are starting to arrive at the destination, the world after the virus. Videos from Israel show us what the new planet might look like at first, with the exhilaration of being at long last free giving way to the deep desire to enjoy life and make up for lost time. Nightclubs in Tel Aviv reopened in March 2021, one year after they were ordered to close. On May 9, Israel reported only eight new cases, a figure taking us back to when the disease was an exotic occurrence. In the United Arab Emirates, where I now live and, after Israel, the country with the second fastest vaccination campaign in the world, tourists and travelers arrive each day from the five continents searching for normality and a place to which all can travel with fewer restrictions. When I arrived at the beginning of the year and a friend walked me through the Dubai International Financial Centre, I nodded with genuine obeisance for the place. It was mostly the feeling of witnessing human life again, landing in an inhabited planet again. The shops and easy money quickly became as insufferable as they have always been.

I have started to think of Dubai as a kind of Casablanca, a free city where pandemic exiles can congregate. Other countries are catching up in their vaccination campaigns and will soon join us at the end of our space odyssey: "Oh what joy, in the open air freely to breathe again! Up here alone is life! The dungeon is a grave."

In May, spirits brand Hennessy said it was expecting a liquor renaissance as consumers splashed out on pricier drinks in a quest for celebration. "Some call it the revenge of pleasure," chief executive Philippe Schaus mused.[3] Government data in the United States shows that millions of Americans aged 55 or older are contemplating retirement years earlier because of the pandemic. The vivid brush with disease and death seems to have helped them reconsider the commitment to climbing the corporate ladder.[4] As Mike Bloomberg put it at the Johns Hopkins University Commencement in May 2021, "whatever you do tonight and tomorrow, and for the rest of your lives: Do it like the world may lock down again tomorrow."

When the futurist architect and thinker R. Buckminster Fuller created the image of the Earth as a spaceship, he wanted to underline that we live in a welcoming planet where everything can be made to serve our interests. "Our little Spaceship Earth is only eight thousand miles in diameter, which is almost a negligible dimension in the great vastness of space."[5] As Fuller noted, the spaceship is so extraordinarily well designed that it took us until very recently to even notice we were on board a ship. So perfectly designed that it is able to keep life regenerating on board by accessing energy from another spaceship, the Sun, traveling at just the right distance from us.

We were lucky with our planet, although luck is not really the word. And obviously, the technological imperative cannot consist in using our planetary spaceship in such a way that we risk impairing or even destroying its operating systems. The technological imperative is to think of our own planet as a complex machine that must be kept in order if we are to survive the journey. The spaceship came without an instruction manual, so we had to use science, which is just a way to reverse engineer the planet, but for Fuller the basic work of science is one of preservation and regeneration.

The Biosphere 2, a project inspired by Fuller and built between 1987 and 1991, was originally meant to demonstrate the viability of closed ecological systems to support and maintain human life, a substitute for Biosphere 1, the Earth itself. A crew of eight humans lived inside the fully enclosed structure for two years, going gradually insane in the process. Oxygen levels decreased faster than anticipated, reaching a hazardous threshold. Extra food had to be smuggled in, against all the rules, and group morale collapsed.[6] The experiment was supposed to announce a future world where humanity lived in harmony with nature. It turned out to make a very different point, one that now looks eerily prophetic. If humanity must take care of its common home because it is finite and resources limited, what lies beyond its walls? It must be a hostile environment of some kind to which the most reasonable response is the one tried by the "biospherians" and now so personal and familiar to all of us: a strict lockdown.

Singapore has taken the concept of the pandemic spaceship to its logical conclusion. Its bubble facility for business travelers allows guests to stay in hotel-like rooms, have meals delivered to a cubbyhole outside their door and to conduct business meetings with other travelers or even Singaporeans. Located in a convention center five minutes from Changi Airport, it plans to host 1,300 travelers by the end of the year. In the meeting rooms designed to host outside guests, the two groups are separated by an air-tight glass panel, and each side of the room has its own ventilation system. The boardroom includes a document transfer box equipped with ultraviolet lighting for disinfection so that the two groups can pass documents back and forth.[7]

I use the image of the spaceship in this sense. By imagining human life as taking place within a large spaceship, we learn that the best image for our natural environment is not the pleasant greenery of the countryside, or even the flooded plain, the creeping weed or the locusts of the desert, but empty space, a medium fundamentally indifferent to life. Perhaps one day we can make physical nature as safe and welcoming as our artificial spaceship, but that can only happen after it has been mastered or controlled by human technology. Remember how in the movie *The Martian* Matt Damon's character is able to grow potatoes on Mars? Well, he does not grow them on Mars but in an artificial surface habitat, the Hab. The line between human technology and the external world remains valid. For the time being, the imperative is to remain vigilant.

As an image for the pandemic, the void or emptiness of the space age is illuminating for a second and more important reason. In some sense, the virus was a return to nature, opening up every political regime to the challenges posed by a hostile environment, a prelude to many other natural crises in our future. What it could not do was return us to the time lost in the past, when nature, under the guidance of a benevolent intelligence, could provide instruction for human life. A mimetic view regards the world as having a given order and a given meaning and sees human beings as required to discover their meaning and conform themselves to it.[8] That is no longer the way we regard the world. We are builders, even when our buildings collapse or our cities are buried in sand and dust. The nature which has suddenly irrupted into normal life is pure negation, the danger of the void. Every country, every civilization was forced to recognize in the pandemic the sudden possibility of loss. Ways of living and achievements that we regarded as final and safe were exposed as fragile and perhaps temporary, in danger of being destroyed or engulfed by the emptiness. The work of civilization was revealed as never fully finished or even protected from the ravages of a hostile environment.

The obvious fragility of the global order placed us face to face with the void, the "eternal silence of these infinite spaces," to use a famous sentence from Pascal. The second part of the great lesson is that we are not alone in empty, infinite space: we have the power of technology to help us survive and prosper. As I continued to think about what the pandemic means for the future of humanity, I became attracted to the image of life in the space age. This book tries to explain why it is much more than a metaphor.

The German legal theorist Carl Schmitt, who died in 1985 at the age of 96, has risen at times to take the role of interpreter of the current pandemic. What he saw—and what has been confirmed by events now very familiar to us all—is that a moment of great danger to the state or to public safety cannot conform to preexisting rules and procedures. The precise details of an emergency cannot be anticipated or spelled out. But Schmitt failed to realize that there is a response to this predicament. The way to prepare for the emergency is to develop our powers of reaction well in advance. The war against nature will last longer than was hoped. And if that is true, our approach to technology needs to change.

The pandemic was a test. Covid saw through what nations say about themselves and revealed what they truly are. Like individuals, governments and regimes can survive or persevere in ways that tell you very little about their capacities. Ability is only evident in action, and action is far from being a constant. In normal times, routine is king. Impersonal rules and procedures may be applied more or less automatically, with little need for decisive action, because nothing will happen in its absence. But when an emergency strikes—an event outside the realm of the ordinary—then rules are useless, and one must return to the original spring of action, understood as a test against the world, with a necessarily uncertain outcome.

In one of the most intriguing tales in *Don Quixote*, we read about a young man who, married to a beautiful woman of high birth, cannot help thinking that her virtue is not as real as her beauty. It has not been tested. The only true virtue is that which has been forced to prove itself. As he puts it to his best friend, "what thanks are due to a woman for being good if nobody is asking her to be bad?" He wants his wife to be put to the test, pursued by temptation and offered the opportunity to resist it. His friend tries to dissuade him, and his arguments are the very image of reason, but, when everything has been considered, not powerful enough. This earnest friend tells him that it is a symptom of a rash mind to put something dear at stake in the way he plans to do. If someone had a diamond which every expert agreed was true and perfect, would it be reasonable to place it between anvil and hammer, to deal it blow after blow in order to see if it was truly as excellent as we think? If the stone passes the test, it will not become any more excellent than it already is. And if it is destroyed, all is lost, and through our own fault. It is inappropriate, he says in a striking formulation, to perform "experiments on truth itself." His friend listens in silence. He knows the danger, but he also knows that truth is not the same as assuming something to be true.

It was easy to think of this tale during the worst months of the pandemic. We had such perfect societies. But they had not been tested.

The tale, needless to say, has nothing to do with female modesty and all to do with the relation between reason and society. What Cervantes is raising is the possibility that our most sacred beliefs are accepted out of habit and convention rather than their intrinsic value. The Enlightenment in Europe was a questioning or a denial of dogmas or practices whose truth no one was allowed to doubt. Everywhere in politics, the individual found divine rights, established privileges, sanctified tyrannies armed with oppressive power. Against the rule of the existing religious and political order, the modern age stood as an experiment on truth itself. As Sri Aurobindo writes, every claim of authority and every sacred truth was put to the test:

> But is it really so? How shall I know that this is the truth of things and not superstition and falsehood? When did God command it, or how do I know that this was the sense of His command and not your error or invention, or that the book on which you found yourself is His word at all, or that He has ever spoken His will to mankind? This immemorial order of which

you speak, is it really immemorial, really a law of Nature or an imperfect result of Time and at present a most false convention? And of all you say, still I must ask, does it agree with the facts of the world, with my sense of right, with my judgment of truth, with my experience of reality?[9]

In the tales of adventure that so attracted Don Quixote, the hero actually sets out without a task or mission. He seeks adventures. What are these? At first glance, they are the sort of perilous encounters with other knights by which he may prove his courage. They are moments outside the ordinary, accidents—but accidents one actively pursues. Usually, they take place in a hidden forest or some other extraordinary landscape in order to stress their unusual and even supernatural essence. There is no social and political context for these adventures, no organized joust, no sacred realm to be defended against the infidels. Here the feudal ethos serves no political function; it serves no practical reality at all. It has become a game, a trial of triumph and loss. In one of these romances, we hear a knight in the court of King Arthur tell us about the time when he came across an ugly and hideous peasant who claimed to watch over the beasts of the woods. Asked what sort of man he is and what he does there, the knight answers that he seeks what he cannot find, "adventures, to test my courage and my strength."

Very few people would willingly set out in search of dangerous and unexpected events, outside the realm of ordinary life, for the sole purpose of testing their prowess and ability. And yet these events do happen, and continue to happen, and they do test us in a way that nothing else can. With their usual detachment and severity, both Albert Camus and Antonin Artaud compared the general result of a plague to the essence of art. Plagues impel us to see ourselves as we are, making the masks fall and divulging our hidden flaws. They shake off the dullness of routine and reveal their dark powers to human beings, urging them to take a more heroic stand in the face of destiny than they would have assumed without it. "In theatre, as in the plague," wrote Artaud, "there is a kind of strange sun, an unusually bright light by which the difficult, even the impossible, suddenly appears to be our natural medium."[10]

The pandemic was a test for every country and every political system because it placed them before something that could not be interpreted or subsumed under their own governing principles. It was a brute fact, still free of interpretation. And it called for action, which is not only the measure of human beings but the measure of their collective life as well. Once action becomes urgent and unavoidable, every political virtue or flaw comes to the surface.

When the epidemic started, subtle changes of political climate and mores that political thinkers used to write about were once again a topic of intense discussion. Were some countries too individualistic? Did they place rights over duties in a way that made it impossible to adopt a collective response to common threats? Or were they too crude in their political responses, too captured by political myth in a way that made it difficult to deal with scientific facts? Later, when vaccines became central to the discussion, we wondered if the ability to take risky decisions in the absence of full information might not be a virtue after all. Perhaps there were important cultural factors, but then the political response was no less colored by cultural differences.

Now it has to be said that some of the most impressive results in the effort to defeat the pandemic came at first from what could roughly be called the Confucian cosmopolis. Singapore flirted with disaster once or twice but quickly recovered. Vietnam showed a remarkable ability to mobilize society against the virus, and South Korea was the early trailblazer in conducting massive testing and building testing clinics that could detect coronavirus cases in minutes, a notable advance in the initial stages of the pandemic. Do these facts illustrate the benefits of a moral system that emphasizes duties before rights and places high value on the propriety of customs, measures and rules as defined by the larger community? In the rival cosmopolis we call the West, the normal or default reaction was one of incredulity and complacency. Many Western democracies were in time quite capable of adopting strict measures, but they always adopted them in the expectation of quickly returning to normal—the pandemic must not really be happening—and many commentators and public officials kept insisting that the greatest danger came not from the virus but from an exaggerated reaction to it. "Most of all, I was concerned about public panic," New York governor Andrew Cuomo wrote. On February 15, chief medical advisor Anthony Fauci told an interviewer that the flu was a bigger threat.

In early March 2020, I received an email from a Chinese university informing me that a conference planned for May would still go ahead. It did not, obviously, but the author of the message took the opportunity to make the point that, by the time the conference did take place, China would be much safer than Europe or America. That was entirely correct. She concluded with the pronouncement that the coronavirus had shown the Chinese model to be superior to the Western one. Chinese authorities complain that the epidemic has been politicized by those wanting to score points against the regime in China, but they were doing exactly the same and from the very beginning. Coming at a time of geopolitical rivalry, the pandemic provided the perfect backdrop for a renewed clash of civilizations.

TRAVELS WITH THE VIRUS

I spent the first few weeks of the coronavirus outbreak on a journey through Asia, part of a professional trip of conferences, lectures, business meetings and literary festivals. At the time, traveling in Asia seemed somewhat imprudent, like tempting the beast by walking right into its cave. I was in China just before Christmas, but do not remember any mention of the virus already spreading in Wuhan. Things had changed when I landed in Pakistan after the New Year. On January 9, 2020, Chinese authorities publicly confirmed reports of an outbreak. Pakistan, whose friendship with China is said to be "higher than the Himalayas and deeper than the deepest sea," hosts a very large Chinese community, but security concerns have increasingly separated them from the larger society. By the second week of January, the Chinese in Pakistan were starting to head home for the lunar New Year. Most would not return, so there was little chance they could bring the virus back with them. The first two cases of Covid-19 in Pakistan were reported in Islamabad and Karachi on February 26. Both patients had traveled from Iran, which by then had become the new epicenter of the looming pandemic. The connection to China, so visible in the news and political intrigue, turned out to be less significant. I suspect we often miss how globalization works on different levels and at different paces. Chinese construction workers in Pakistan do not fly back and forth between the two countries, like Italian or German businessmen do.

On January 20, the day President Xi Jinping made his first public statement on the coronavirus, I was crossing the border between Pakistan and India. With me was Venki Ramakrishnan, a biologist and co-winner of the Nobel Prize in Chemistry in 2009. We had spoken together at a public event in Lahore. The outbreak never came up, not at the event or in conversation. Traveling from Lahore to Amritsar, my thoughts turned to the thick smog from stubble burning covering what seemed the whole of Punjab. The twin cities of Lahore and Amritsar, once part of the same world and now separated by an impenetrable barrier, might have provided an apt image for the future awaiting us, but back then the virus was still a story happening somewhere else. It did not take long for the situation to change.

On January 23, President Xi imposed a strict cordon sanitaire on Wuhan and three other cities. Two days later, as I waited in Jaipur for the short flight to Agra, I was joined in the terminal by a crowd of Chinese tourists, all of them heavily masked. One young man wore a giant black elastomeric respirator, looking distinctively cyberpunk. Did he know something we did not?

A week later I was at the Indira Gandhi Airport in Delhi, getting ready for a flight to Kathmandu. When I reached the security line, the person behind me was none other than Ramakrishnan, whom I had last seen at the Pakistan border ten days earlier. As we placed our bags in trays and lay them on the conveyor belt, he told me that there was nothing to fear. The odds of getting the virus were minimal and the odds of dying from it if you got it were, again, negligible.

I waited for Ramakrishnan at the other end of the security check and asked him what he thought the odds were of two people meeting in Pakistan and then by chance running into each other in India ten days later. He laughed. It is my last memory of laughing about the virus.

Panic had started to spread, and I was not immune. For the next leg of the journey, I had finally decided to buy a mask. The pharmacy in the Aerocity in Delhi had none left, so the attendants suggested I took some vitamins instead. When I relayed the story to the concierge at my hotel, he handed me a small bag with about half a dozen surgical masks. "Do not tell anyone," he whispered.

Looking back, what strikes me is how much of my days was already being changed by the coronavirus, and how the most vivid memories of those travels ended up being those that better expressed what life would become. My mind was looking and thinking in a new way. Why else would I remember the name of the 98.4° pharmacy in Delhi? 98.4 degrees Fahrenheit, the normal temperature for a healthy human being. Even the name acquired an ironic meaning.

That moment, of course, announced everything that was yet to come: the desperate struggle for medical supplies, the search for makeshift treatments and the impending sense of doom. More powerful than the fear was the anxiety that one wrong decision or a careless approach could cost one dearly, and worst of all would be the gesture of blaming ourselves later, if tragedy arrived. It felt like a lot of weight on our shoulders, and walking back to my hotel, I looked at the passersby and was sure they felt it too. The exchange with the concierge reminded me how unfair and unforgiving this renewed struggle for existence would inevitably become.

At this point, the virus was just an idea. Only in Nepal would I finally arrive in a country with a confirmed case. But what a powerful idea it was.

My time in the Himalayas was no less framed by the virus. On the surface, there were the walks along the Durbar in the three magical cities of the valley, or the trek up to Gorkha with the long lines of pilgrims carrying their animals to be sacrificed, or the majesty of the Annapurna towering over every previous concept of what a mountain looks like. There was all this, yes, and perhaps at another time I would have remembered these places with different feelings. But the mood was shifting. On the drive to the Annapurna I had a bad cough, and there was a chance it was the beginning of an infection picked up among the crowds at the Jaipur Literary Festival. One already felt that Covid was somehow everywhere, that the limits of our freedom and our enjoyment of life were shrinking. Fantastic thoughts entered your mind. Might this be one of those human catastrophes one had only read about? Countries such as Pakistan, India and Nepal seemed so vulnerable to a deadly pandemic, no one in his or her right mind could avoid fearing for the vast mass of mankind left without resources to fight the threat.

A year later, with the appearance of new variants and a higher global virus prevalence, India would be entering its deadly second wave. By April 2021, the outbreak had topped 300,000 new cases a day. The sudden wave came after India relaxed restrictions and the idea grew that perhaps it had reached something approaching collective immunity. The images filling our screens will be hard to forget: the scramble to get oxygen, the social media posts pleading for help, the sick dying in hospital parking lots, the crematoria running for so long without a break that metal parts began to melt. Everything seemed to be on sale on the black market, from oxygen and the drug remdesivir, to hospital beds and ambulances. Denied even cremation pyres for their parents and relatives, many had no alternative but to tie the corpses to the tops of their cars and drive to crematoria in neighboring cities. Wood for the pyres was sold at ten or twenty times the normal price. In one case, a grieving young woman—the youngest of three daughters—suddenly jumped onto the funeral pyre of her father, who had died after contracting Covid, while he was being cremated. Although quickly pulled out by those attending the funeral, she sustained around 70% burn injuries.[11]

Forced to revert to their personal networks or to appeal to strangers on the internet, Indians suddenly realized how much they had neglected the task of statecraft. The pandemic identified a fundamental weakness, common to the Hindus of the past described in the famous Patan trilogy by K. M. Munshi: the lack of a state. How to finally overcome the legacies of the colonial past? Does India have the architects of a modern and successful state? Hindol Sengupta pointed out how the second wave of the disease "taught the rich and the upwardly mobile that they cannot escape into a bubble bought by their relative prosperity while the poor suffer indignities caused by a fundamental lack of infrastructure and resources." Indian society acted in everything like a modern society. Only there was no modern state on which to rely, and, without the protective environment of the state, the free and dynamic form of Indian society looked like an act of suicide. "You can no longer buy yourself out of this crisis. And there is nowhere to fly off to because most countries have bars on visitors from places with a major surge in virus outbreak." Covid was a moment of truth. It could also become a moment of salvation.[12] Manoj Joshi called the April wave a return to medieval society, the breakdown of the structures of a modern state.[13] Personal networks can help if there is a hospital bed or an oxygen cylinder available, but what happens when they are not available anywhere, when the need is to change the existing conditions? As the pandemic progressed, it became clear to me that the question towards which it pointed was the modern conquest of nature, the passage from nature to civilization and the danger of a relapse.

On one of my last days in Kathmandu I visited the Pashupatinath Temple on the banks of the Bagmati, and every other image of Nepal receded into the background. Now, I know the virus was the reason the visit had such a strange effect. There was an obvious coincidence between a place where the visitor is confronted with the dead and the looming threat of a virus reminding us of our common mortality. One body was being washed with river water, wrapped with a white cloth, and sprinkled with flowers. Bodies were burned on the ghats and the smell of their charred flesh filled the air we breathed. At the time I may have thought that none of this seemed like a good idea. Had these people perhaps died of Covid? But what is a good idea during a pandemic? Allowing people to die alone, preventing their loved ones from being present and then quickly making their bodies disappear? In Pashupatinath they were not prepared for a virus, but they were prepared for death, and better prepared than any of us would ever be. The pandemic would in time turn into a similar lesson, a preparation for death and a call to a fuller life. The virus would return us to an older world where death could no longer be hidden from view. In that world, Pashupatinath no longer stood out as a relic of the past.

I left on an empty night flight and the journey felt like a leap in time. In Singapore they seemed to know everything in advance. For the first time, the virus actually changed my plans, with a large lecture in Singapore being canceled and replaced by smaller meetings, in accordance with the new containment measures. It was an interesting experience to visit the city at the beginning of the pandemic because it offered an early template of what authorities should do to fight it. Over the next few months I would return to my week in Singapore and be tortured by the constant reminder it provided that things could be very different.

There were signs of the virus wherever you looked. Your temperature was constantly measured, testing was already pervasive and new cases were plotted against every available data point in order to anticipate the potential progression of the epidemic. During a meeting with the dean of a Singapore university, he suddenly excused himself, leaving the room to take his temperature and upload photographic evidence of the result to a dedicated website. Despite the high number of cases recorded, there was a sense that things were under control, or at least as much under control as they could possibly be. With the exception of a moment in September, when the virus took over the dormitories of the poorest migrant workers in the city, Singapore has remained in control, using a savvy combination of technology and civic education. By February 2020, the Singapore Health Department was already employing 5,000 contact tracers to identify and stop infection points before they had time to spread: one person per thousand in the whole country. For a large percentage of confirmed cases in Singapore, the first indication they had was a phone call from the health ministry telling them they had possibly been exposed and needed to be tested and isolated. "It was surreal," a British resident explained back in March 2020, describing the moment an unknown number flashed up on her phone. "They asked 'were you in a taxi at 18:47 on Wednesday?' It was very precise. I guess I panicked a bit, I could not think straight."[14] The next day she found out just how serious the officials were. Three people turned up at her door, wearing medical jackets and surgical masks.

When I told Singapore's former civil service chief Peter Ho that I thought China had overreacted to the problem, he politely demurred: "Actually what we learned in 2003 is that you need to overreact to this sort of thing. Better to overreact." There has been a lot of interest in the way the SARS outbreak in 2003 prepared some countries for Covid, but the lessons were more ambiguous. Chinese authorities took longer to react back in December and January, in part because they were following protocols put in place at the time of SARS. We had all been trained to respond to a pandemic where contagion could be limited by the ability to track easily detectable symptoms.

"Better to overreact." As a lesson in pandemic control, it carried two meanings. First, public authorities must stay ahead of the curve. There is no alternative other than making risky projections about the future and framing public policy in response to those projections. As Nicholas Christakis puts it, if a school is prepared to close in a reactive fashion once there is an outbreak in the school, why not close a little earlier and get more of the benefit? After all, if there is community transmission near the school, it is a certainty that it will reach the school before too long. Waiting to implement reactive measures carries all the same burdens with much fewer benefits.[15] During the following year, the authorities in many Western democracies never understood this basic point, insisting on reacting to what they called "the data," by which was meant past data—obviously useless in this case. In retrospect, "speed was probably the most significant factor in determining national outcomes, and just about every nation in the West failed to move quickly enough."[16] Either you react to natural threats as active agents and try to be the first mover, or you regard nature as passive material for your plans. The pandemic exposed how misguided the latter philosophy truly was.

The second meaning refers to the complex reactions of society as a whole. Significant changes were already happening in Singapore as a response to the virus. People kept their distance from each other. You might avoid meeting strangers, even on romantic occasions. Large gatherings were postponed to a more propitious occasion. Elevators were less full. The social organism was alive, changing and adapting in response to a new environment. Here, too, my shock on returning to Europe was to see that practically nothing had changed. East Asians are unfairly accused of being somewhat robotic in their personal habits. Comparing East Asia and Europe during the first few months of the pandemic, I had to wonder if the opposite might not be closer to the truth. The world had changed, but the Italians, French and Spanish continued to follow their most sacred habits to the end.

On the flight from Singapore to Manila, I noticed a new civility between passengers. People kept their distance, and everyone seemed calmer than usual. Why pick a fight about the overhead bins when that could only force you to interact with other human beings? Perhaps it was not obvious at first because it happened so slowly, but normal activity was being suspended, step by step, and new arrangements put in its place. We were getting ready to enter the spaceship and hop into a sleep pod, with everyone frozen in cryogenic sleep until the ship arrived safely at the new planet.

If Singapore was all about planning and preparation, the mood in Manila was one of shock and fear. Most people were wearing a mask, but good ones were not easily available. People used what they could find—a handkerchief, a dirty rag—to cover their mouths. It was mostly the poor who were taking this precaution. Eschewing a mask had become a status symbol, marking the healthy from the unhealthy, the strong from the weak. In the wealthiest parts of Manila, faces were still bare.

Driving towards Manila Bay, I spotted a young man weaving a Vespa through the dangerous traffic. He was carrying a small child on his lap and the child had a tiny mask hanging down his or her face, a talisman against the cruelty and injustice of life in the megacity. Places like Manila cannot be defeated by a virus. They are built like machines to deal with a punishing environment. Most of their people never stop struggling against disease and poverty, and the cities find their energy in that struggle. The pandemic merely reaffirmed their mission. It was no surprise that they came together, emerging even stronger from the challenge.

When I met Secretary of Foreign Affairs Teddy Locsin for lunch at his favorite Spanish restaurant, he was about to leave for a meeting in Laos designed to show support for China. Meanwhile, travel from China had been banned as a result of strong public pressure. Locsin is an astute diplomat. The pandemic had barely arrived in the Philippines, but he knew the challenge facing the country and was already performing a balancing act: balance under pressure. Who could know at that early stage what the country would need, and who might be in a better position to provide it? I was not surprised a year later to see that the Philippines had managed to secure vaccine supplies from everyone, including India and Russia, whom both President Duterte and Locsin had been courting for a few years.

Manila Bay, usually crowded with Chinese expats, felt empty. Next to my hotel, a Chinese restaurant and nightclub had been shuttered. The world had changed since I was in India a month earlier: cities and neighborhoods bustling with Chinese activity had gone quiet, leaving behind an abandoned landscape.

The last leg of my journey took me to Vietnam. On paper, the country should be among the most vulnerable. It has a large Chinese community, and tourists from every continent are constantly arriving in large numbers. Its border in the north is the busiest Chinese border. But Vietnam managed Covid with flying colors. By March 2021, more than a year after the first cases, it had recorded no more than thirty-five deaths in total.

After a few hours in Ho Chi Minh, it was easy to understand why the situation was under control. The outdoorsy lifestyle and the masks against traffic pollution may have helped, but Vietnam had a third weapon in the war against the virus: widespread dread. People took matters into their own hands. The virus invaded your every thought. Already in February—while most of the world was still learning how to pronounce Wuhan—entering a restaurant involved washing your hands with sanitizer, getting your temperature measured and being led by a fully masked hostess to a dark corner. All taxi drivers wore masks and some added gloves to the uniform. Every conversation touched on the coronavirus, every coughing incident was remarked upon and tourists were asked about their provenance.

Many governments spoke of the virus as the "invisible enemy," but Vietnam was unique in taking this metaphor literally. Even when just a handful of cases had been detected, the authorities were already implementing a plan aimed at stopping a large outbreak. During the Tet New Year at the end of January 2020, Prime Minister Nguyễn Xuân Phúc said Vietnam was "declaring war" on the coronavirus. The country was one of the first to impose travel restrictions on China, but not in the spirit of stopping the arrival of the epidemic. The restrictions were just one tool to reduce the spread of an infection everyone assumed was already present in some form. Quarantines were imposed on very large numbers of people, again based on an extremely comprehensive understanding of what a risky contact might be. Remember that even in China, lockdowns of entire cities were adopted only as a last resort. On February 12, Vietnam put an entire town of 10,000 people near Hanoi under quarantine for three weeks, at a time when there were only ten confirmed cases in the whole country.

The pandemic in Vietnam had the structure of an epic fantasy novel, less a matter of public policy than a battle against a potential and invisible threat of which one knows only the dangers.

It is interesting to think that those two weeks in old Saigon were probably the only moment during the pandemic when I was genuinely afraid of catching the virus. The paranoia worked. It worked in my case and it worked for Vietnam, the best performer worldwide in containing Covid. I decided to leave, believing myself to be at the very heart of the coming catastrophe. As it turned out, Vietnam would have been the safest place to spend the whole of 2020. I was at the heart not of the actual catastrophe, but of the fear of catastrophe.

After a few days waiting for my scheduled departure, I finally flew from Singapore to Turkey, leaving half of Asia behind. In Istanbul, in the first two weeks of March, people were visibly concerned. They listened to the news and worried. But daily life continued more or less as before, the restaurants open and many even full. Turks, after all, have a double nature. Like Asians, they never completely trust the future. But like Europeans, they believe in miracles. On the Ides of March, it seemed that Istanbul as a whole believed that Turkey would be the only country in the world to escape the pandemic; the first death was officially reported on March 15, when hundreds of Italians were dying each day. I believed it too, but by then I wanted to believe anything.

FREEDOM AND ITS ENEMIES

The remarkable fact is that both the patterns of daily life and the perceptions of the surrounding reality tended to shift as you moved from country to country. It started to look as if one was moving not between different civilizations but between different planets altogether. Each political regime had its own concept of the external environment. In some places the environment was a placid and beneficial landscape for human beings, fully tamed and put to use. Elsewhere it was an aggressive or secretive enemy against which human beings had to marshal all their physical and mental resources. In the United States it seemed to have vanished altogether, with journalists and politicians busy with the ongoing culture wars or fabulous narratives straight out of a Hollywood production.

After Istanbul, my travels to London and Zurich in the following weeks showed a world where no one was yet ready to care much about the danger or entertain any policy measures to address it. At Heathrow in May— Britain had been since March under what seemed to me a very flexible lockdown—the security guards did not wear masks and laughed loudly when I suggested they might consider it. One surmised in these differences the importance of the political regime, the set of common understandings, often unconscious, around which every society is organized.

That, in a way, was the problem. Every society was following the principles giving it form and life, but nothing could assure you that those principles were the aptest to face the circumstances at hand. Whilst before a society somehow functioned in a vacuum, simply giving expression to its own preferences, it now had to respond to the external environment. That environment was no longer passive, no longer a mere background or landscape. It called for a response. The pandemic exposed this gap between the political regime and the problems of the external world in a way that had not been exposed before. The end time is a time of revelation.

Suddenly, there was a way to compare political regimes that seemed less internal and much more objective. The threat posed by a quickly multiplying virus was not determined by the values espoused in different countries, but driven from the outside and by a common adversary. For Western democracies, it was a delicate moment. Until now they had been powerful enough to export their values worldwide and, in fact, to subject every other regime to their own judgments. The pandemic introduced a standard of a different kind. In some obvious way they were found wanting, even if it is still unclear whether to a greater or lesser extent than their main rivals. One obvious problem was the way liberal democracies reacted by appealing to their routine practices and principles. The emergency was a spur to action, but regrettably to the kind of action they were used to. For example, the commitment to an abstract notion of equality led to policy measures that often seemed more concerned with treating different cases equally than with actually addressing the growth of infection cases. Hence, the general but loose lockdowns, the reluctance to use digital contact tracing and the rather absurd focus on restricting all those activities that could be construed as voluntary. Going to the beach was banned in many places, while public transportation continued to function almost normally. The latter was a much greater danger—beaches were perhaps the safest places one could find—but societies founded on personal choice wanted to fight the pandemic in those areas where personal choice was the dominant factor.

Similarly, the democratic commitment to rules rather than personal power often meant that falsely precise guidelines were blindly imposed and followed, and that clarity and uniformity were invariably preferred to actual results. Our need to fully justify action by politicians and public officials—a basic corollary of the rule of law—tended to reduce the ability to make decisions, which in a moment of emergency can never be fully justified by the data, let alone publicly available knowledge. Younger democracies such as Taiwan and South Korea did much better, not so much because their publics have a stronger collective sense, but because their rules and procedures are less fixed, less ossified and could therefore be adapted to new circumstances. It was not Confucianism but a kind of modernity we have lost in the West. In the end, however, the critical comparison was that between liberal democracies and China. Western democracies were supposed to have done better than an authoritarian regime at fighting a pandemic. They are open and transparent. They have access to the facts without the censoring impulse of the state. They can rely on a committed public. They can correct mistakes. They enjoy a robust public debate from which the best policy decisions can be expected to emerge. So, when China surprised Western observers by quickly reaching faster and superior outcomes in the fight to stop the spread of the virus, an important debate about the roots of its relative success—and its consequences for the ideological conflict between alternatives—quickly became necessary. In a controversial article, the *New York Times* Asia tech columnist Li Yuan argued that while people in China cannot enjoy freedom of speech or freedom from fear, they were, during the pandemic, free to move around and lead a normal life, a "most basic form of freedom" that people living in democracies would envy.[17]

It took a while, of course, for China to reach the kind of normal life Li Yuan was talking about, and the methods were often quite ruthless. One obvious difference was the way China proceeded to mass-quarantine patients with only mild symptoms. We knew almost from the start how infectious the virus could be, even in those who show no symptoms, so China opted to isolate every positive case in large makeshift hospitals converted from offices or stadiums. This way they would not run the risk of passing the virus to family members. Most of the transmission during the worst peaks of the pandemic happened in the household between family members, but in Europe and the United States it remained impossible to impose any kind of separation until a patient was so sick that they had to be moved to a hospital. Perhaps in some cases families were able to preserve the necessary distance at home while a family member recovered. More often, families became one of the main infection vectors, but when a group of Chinese experts advised health authorities in Milan to follow their approach, they quickly found out it could not be done in Europe, not by political fiat. In China, a Pakistani baby who arrived on a flight and tested positive was separated from his parents and held for medical observation for more than a month.

When the Chinese authorities wanted to stop the spread of the virus, they relied on lockdowns. Western democracies went on to apply their own versions of a lockdown, but they differed markedly from the Chinese model. In Europe or the United States, there was at different times a general order not to leave your home—more common in Europe than America—but I have been the subject of these orders more than once, and they were never to be interpreted literally. An order to stay at home meant simply that you needed a good excuse to leave, or, more often, no excuse at all, because police officers would be interested in more obviously social activities than a lonely stroll. In China, those orders were to be followed to the letter. Even if the cases of people having their apartment doors nailed shut were clearly the exception—but official seals were common—officials and volunteers from the residential committees, the most grassroots level of the Communist Party, did seal off buildings and erect barricades outside residential compounds in affected areas to make sure no one could enter or leave. In some cases, one family member might be allowed to leave to buy groceries. In the most critical moments of the epidemic, even that possibility was fore-closed. Delivery services or the residential communities would leave a bag with food outside your door, keeping everyone inside their homes for weeks on end. In Beijing and other cities less affected by virus outbreaks, those committees were still camped outside compounds, taking every resident's temperature as they went in and out and stopping them from entertaining guests at home.

These residential committees were doing serious work. Before the pandemic—as I witnessed during my year living by the Lama Temple in Beijing—they were present in the small affairs of the hutongs or residential alleys, sometimes helping solve conflicts between neighbors. Now they were entrusted with a national mission of the highest importance and were punished for the smallest mistakes. Peter Hessler tells the story of an official assigned to a compound with 1,136 units. For two days he knocked on every single unit, questioning residents and checking their health status. He missed one apartment, the very apartment containing the only coronavirus case in the residential district, and was forced to apologize in public. His career never recovered. At some point, the Chinese state press reported that fifty-three members of residential committees lost their lives while working to control the virus.[18]

While public transport was left operational in European and American cities—reducing the frequency of buses and the subway only made social distancing impracticable—in the worst hit Chinese cities transportation services were completely suspended. In Wuhan, limited bus routes were not resumed until the end of March 2020, nine weeks into the lockdown.[19] Since most Wuhan residents did not have a car, countless people infected with the coronavirus ended up traipsing all over the city in the wind and rain looking for a hospital that would admit them, a haunting scene described by the writer Fang Fang in her contemporaneous diary. Later, all vehicles were prohibited from circulating in downtown Wuhan.

Hessler notes that Chinese officials never depended very much on mask use, social distancing or other forms of individual judgment to reduce infections: "Instead, the strategy was to enforce a lockdown until the virus was eliminated." Later, mass testing was used, with local authorities often succeeding in testing a whole major city in just a few days. The government did not trust individuals to set the terms of their own behavior during the worst moments of the crisis, but it did require people to work hard as elements of the mobilized social organism fighting the pandemic. It was Chinese society as a whole responding to the pandemic, not an authoritarian government. Even discounting the myriad of volunteers and swashbuckling business dealers, there was the army of home delivery services, what some Chinese call "little delivery boys" (快递小哥), a sector where China is the undisputed world leader. "Home delivery played a very important role amid the coronavirus outbreak," Hu Xingdou, a political economist in Beijing, told the *South China Morning Post*. "To some extent, it prevented people from starving, especially in cases when local governments took extreme measures to isolate people."[20] Think about it as the harmony of market and state, the former rendering the "extreme measures" of the latter possible in the first place.

While the emphasis was on defeating a natural enemy, it is far from clear who had the upper hand. Human beings were both masters and slaves. Their efforts were applauded as cogs in the social mechanism, but they were also part of the undifferentiated nature, devoid of judgment or will, which was to be brought under control. When people such as the whistleblower doctor, Wenliang Li, dared to exercise their own judgment, they were unhesitatingly punished.

Fang Fang refers poignantly to the same paradox when she remarks on being shocked to hear a Chinese writer talk about a resounding victory over the virus:

> I was speechless. Take a look at Wuhan! Take a look at the entire country! Millions of people are living in fear, thousands of people are hospitalized with their lives hanging by a thread, countless families have been destroyed. Where is this win? Where is this victory?[21]

In a later passage, she dwells on a newspaper report of the death of a patient in Wuhan named Xiao Xianyou. Just before he passed away, he had left behind a kind of testament that was only two lines long or just eleven Chinese characters. However, when the newspaper ran a story about his death, they used the following headline: "Seven Final Words That Left Everyone in Tears." Those seven words were: *I donate my body to the nation.* There were four words after that, which the newspaper omitted: *what about my wife?* Perhaps the editors thought the private and quiet love one man has for his wife was of no historical significance...

Imagine, then, the human being as a circle or, better yet, a spiral. As he or she acts and builds, they themselves are the object of their power; only now there are two human beings, a higher one who builds and a lower object who is molded and formed according to a plan. When you exalt the human, what you exalt is that higher being, but you feel very little for its lower creature, until you realize that little by little the acting subject has been turned into sculpted matter, and the spiral turned upside down.

Jiang Hui, a top executive at the Chinese company Shuwei Media Technology, described the process as the "digitization of people." He had in mind the control of community outbreaks with the help of Big Data and the use of a wristband tracking the movements of people under quarantine, but the concept can be used more widely. "What we are doing essentially is to digitize people and provide services based on the labels, location, and other information that we attach to people," he explained.[22] Both processes can be understood in the same way. On the one hand, human beings get reinterpreted as infection points in a global system where flows are continuously tracked. On the other, workers in the new economy become digital subjects; only as such can they be protected from a dangerous environment.

The victory, or more accurately the tragedy of the Enlightenment first manifests itself when the creations of the spirit take on a life of their own. This kind of externalization has happened in various circumstances historically, as when religion becomes a limit to the very creativity of the human spirit that gave it birth. Cultural objects detach from their creators and acquire their own "needs." An endless stream of commodities is produced by an industrial and economic system, which has at some point started to follow its own laws, seemingly beyond our control. "The infinitely growing stock of the objectified mind makes demands on the subject, arouses faint aspirations in it, strikes it with feelings of its own insufficiency and helplessness, entwines it into total constellations from which it cannot escape as a whole without mastering its individual elements," observed the sociologist Georg Simmel.[23] Dead products and a deadly logic, set apart from the febrile rhythm of life itself and its constant renewal. Sri Aurobindo pointed out that the modern discoveries of science were simultaneously the triumph of the individual and his or her announced death. A triumph because truth was now the product of the free search for the fundamental structure of the world. The death of individualism because the establishment of these universal laws "seems to lead logically to the suppression of that very individual freedom which made the discovery and the attempt at all possible." The result to which it points and to which it still seems irresistibly to be driving us is a new ordering of society by rational laws and the rule of experts.[24] During the pandemic, somber characters we had never seen before were put in charge of every detail of our lives, including whether we should be allowed to meet with loved ones. And so it happened.

Industries and sciences, arts and organizations: all impose their content and their pace of development on individuals, regardless of, or even contrary to, their wishes or needs. The relentless objectification of the human spirit proceeds apace: a photograph copies what before could exist only in the human mind. But how far can the logic of objectification be taken? Only recently have we started to ask whether the human being might be entirely replaced by an artificial construct, a synthetic being taking its place alongside other human creations. But then, with human beings replaced by this synthetic construct, who exactly would be in charge? It would have to be technology itself, represented by a technological version of the human or, in brief, a human machine. Thus, the living question in China today: how to ensure that the individual is not fully replaced by technology? Is it too late to dream of a modern society that has all kinds of wondrous new technologies at its disposal—and never ceases to invent new ones—while remaining fully committed to the question of what human life is for and how human beings should live, without allowing that question to be answered by technology?

In our time, this discussion normally turns on the possibilities of genetic engineering and human enhancement. We are troubled by the idea that human beings, while reaching their ultimate perfection as masters of nature, will themselves be turned into manufactured objects. The dialectic of Enlightenment would then reach its foretold conclusion. The transformation of human beings from subjects into objects entails their disappearance as genuine sources of action and autonomous judgment. But genetic engineering is too narrow a focus in this context. Other areas exist where the displacement of the grown by the made is arguably happening faster, and with more visible consequences. The pandemic seems an obvious example. The digitization of people is one dimension of the problem. The transformation of the human into a dangerous animal—a cause of infection and even death for its own species—provides a darker angle.

One comparison that often struck me between the way China and Western democracies dealt with the threat was this: China seemed determined to do what was necessary to obtain results in the most direct and obvious way, while Western democracies stopped to ask a previous question: what is the proper or adequate way for a society such as ours to act in order to fight the virus? I think there are two ways to look at this odd intrusion of a theoretical question at a moment of peril. First, you could regard it as an excess of ideology. Everything, even survival, has become an ideological question and under these circumstances effective action becomes impossible. But you could also regard it as the deliberate resistance to instinctive reactions, or the vague remembrance of a kind of philosophical questioning stopping us from going through life with little or no thought. Be that as it may, it illustrated an obvious difference between the way Chinese and European authorities approached the pandemic, helping to explain the relative failure of the latter.

On March 12, 2020, the number of new coronavirus cases in Wuhan dropped below ten for the first time, with most districts in the city down to zero. The next day the World Health Organization announced that Europe was now the epicenter of the pandemic. As the announcement was made, many countries in Africa and Asia were imposing strict restrictions on the arrival of flights and visitors from Europe. It felt like a great historical reversal, one full of irony. Suddenly Europeans were being kept away, they who for so long fortified their borders against all the dangers—real or imagined— arriving from the developing world.

A year later, in March 2021, the European Union was again the epicenter of a third wave of the pandemic, while its vaccination campaign floundered against all expectations. The crisis was, before everything else, a public health crisis, but it also reflected profound changes in the way the continent sees itself. Many of these changes have been taking place for a while. Previous moments such as the debt or refugee crises can be linked with the ongoing epidemic as part of a larger pattern, but the coronavirus has made everything more visible and certainly more tragic. It seems clear to me that the extent of the outbreak in Europe is directly connected to subtle questions of cultural identity, some of which I want to discuss here.

In an interview published at the beginning of the first wave of the pandemic in Spain, the director of a hospital in Madrid was unusually forthcoming. Still traumatized by the images of the emergency care unit where he works, Santiago Moreno confessed that "we have sinned from too much confidence." As he explained it, everyone in Spain thought an epidemic such as the novel coronavirus could spread in a place like China, but not "in a country like ours."[25] It is simple really. People in Europe still think of China as a developing country. When news started to arrive of the outbreak in Wuhan, they imagined filthy Chinese markets and hospitals, they thought of the spitting and the lack of doctors, and they trembled. They feared for the Chinese people, not for themselves. This perception explains why, as mainstream opinion lambasted China for mismanaging the outbreak, there was remarkably little concern that the mismanagement could have consequences for Europe and other parts of the developed world. There was effectively no planning or preparation.

I should note here that the very limited number of people who first became alert to the great danger facing the world—and who grew increasingly angry at the lack of seriousness in Europe or America—were almost invariably those with some knowledge of contemporary China. If you know what progress China has made and how the country is now ahead of the West on many dimensions of what constitutes a modern society, you are very unlikely to shrug with indifference when Chinese authorities lock down a major megapolis.

It was serious, but no one in Europe took it seriously. The unbearable lightness of being. At the beginning of March 2020, the Spanish government actively encouraged all Spaniards to go on the streets and join dozens of very large marches for gender equality. When asked about the infection hazard, one minister laughed. The images of those marches have acquired a tangible, pungent horror. You see them against the backdrop of the 100,000 deaths since then, and the laughter, the hugs and the claps from the marches stand as a lasting monument to human folly.

Spain was not alone in this. Also in early March, a French municipality organized a large convention of Smurfs, the little blue creatures who live in mushroom-shaped houses in the forest, made famous by a Belgian comic series. According to the mayor of the small town where the convention took place, "we figured that a bit of fun would do us all good at the moment."[26] A few days later, after President Macron publicly advised the French to be more cautious in their daily lives, nothing had changed and the images of the crowded esplanades in Paris forced his government to coercively enforce their closure. One year later, a new harsh lockdown would be decreed. "They have forgotten nothing and they have learned nothing."

At the time of the Madrid marches and the Smurf convention, I was returning from my journey in Asia and could not help noticing the contrast. In Singapore or Vietnam, people were dramatically changing their behavior to adapt to the coronavirus. They were going out less, avoiding large groups, taking turns on the elevator and, of course, wearing masks everywhere, even if perhaps they looked less elegant in them. The idea that they would organize a Smurf convention to have a little fun is enough to make one, well... laugh.

All this is well and good. It might be a cultural difference. The problem, of course, is that it probably explains why Europe has over the long months of the pandemic so often stood at its epicenter. And it carries a dark foreboding for the future of a continent which seems to be poorly prepared for a world beyond normal times.

The reasons for this cultural difference can, I believe, be explained through history and psychology. The sense of uncertainty and of the fragility of human life that you still see in Asia is easy to explain if poverty and disease are still everyday occurrences, or, at most, two or three generations in the past. Often, that historical experience is reflected in public institutions: the lack of advanced social security and public healthcare systems forces Asians to contemplate in their daily lives the possibility that their world might suddenly collapse. In Europe, the general psychology too often reflects the ideology of development, the idea that the most serious threats to individual happiness have been definitively conquered. Why worry about an epidemic if you have excellent public hospitals available, more or less for free? What no one considered was that a virus could bring this perfect system to the point of breakdown. We had such perfect societies. But they had not been tested.

Of course, Europeans have their own nightmares and demons. But remember that the tragedy of the World Wars has been interpreted in political terms. They are a reminder of the dangers of nationalism and imperialism. The practical import of Europe's recent history is to confirm our conviction in the rightness of our values, not to force us to doubt ourselves. And even the bloody history of the twentieth century in Europe has not changed the fact that we look at the world from what we think is a central position to which others can only aspire. Europeans have been taught by the whole course of modern history to think that they can guide or at least influence the rest of the world, while being protected from events originating elsewhere. Would it be wrong to think that the new coronavirus is an event of unparalleled significance precisely because, for the first time, this worldview is shown to be unsustainable?

Everything looks so different now. The collective instinct common in other societies and the excessive precautions taken in response to the dangers of a pandemic and other fantastic threats—these emotions which the developed world used to regard as atavisms of less advanced societies take on a new meaning. Perhaps they are less atavisms than evolutionarily apt instincts that help the human species survive in a hostile environment. The belief that we had conquered nature once and for all? Perhaps premature. The feeling that science can be replaced with postmodernism? A dangerous delusion. The permanent suspicion directed against technology? You get the point.

In a penetrating piece published when Italy entered its long national nightmare, the Italian journalist Mattia Ferraresi argued that the fundamental failure in Italy— the first European country to succumb to the pandemic—was not a lack of testing or slow political action but a social and collective failure: people just did not take the coronavirus seriously enough to even slightly adapt their habits. It was a brave argument. It would be much easier to criticize the government for errors of action or inaction, rather than risk being accused of blaming the victims. But what Ferraresi saw and could not repress was something else: the radical incapacity on the part of the Italian public to adapt to the possibility of a terrible outcome, an outcome discounted by everyone until it was really too late. "I and many other Italians just did not see the need to change our routines for a threat we could not see." Even though he had accumulated a lot of information on the virus, Ferraresi writes that he lacked what you might call "moral knowledge."[27] He knew about the virus, but the issue was not affecting his actions. The coronavirus has already shown that we need to relearn how to live in the world. A painful lesson it could be.

THE SINGULARITY

In a strange way, Americans could not have been better prepared for the disaster. For decades they had been consuming high doses of dystopian novels, dark miniseries and blockbuster disaster movies. When the coronavirus struck, many felt they had entered a fictional world, a phenomenon possibly explained by the dominance of the disaster genre among the most popular fictional creations of contemporary America. But that is the logic of the disaster movie. It is a form of art, a human creation, that portrays its very negation in the highly contrived enactment of untamed nature. At the same time, art and human invention win in the end because the natural disaster is quickly downgraded to the role of pretext or occasion. What the movie portrays is the human drama, the conflict, the virtues and perversions hidden in the human soul, while the disaster itself becomes something distant and formless, at times practically disappearing into mere suggestion.

If you opened a newspaper in Spain, France or Italy during 2020, everything was about infection curves, vaccines, viral mutations and endless pages of statistics and graphs. In America things took a different turn. Mere weeks into the deadly pandemic, America had already constructed large, archetypal myths by which to make sense of events. On the left, Trump as Aztec priest. Opening up the country appeared to many like a sacrificial act, the immolation of thousands of lives at the altar of a deified capitalist economy. On the right, and starting in the last week of April, China was being blamed for bringing the virus into the country. Like the serpent in the Book of Genesis, China had lied or at least deceived with cunning and malice. Like the serpent, it had wilfully destroyed the innocence of American life. Unlike the serpent, China could be sued or otherwise forced to offer reparations. On April 27, Trump suggested at a White House news conference that the United States would seek hundreds of billions of dollars in damages from China.

For others, the coronavirus crisis should be interpreted as an instance of dystopian fiction. Where is the president in *Blade Runner*? Nowhere, of course. Kelsey Atherton argued that science fiction dystopias are the logical culmination of a political project designed to fundamentally limit what governments can do.[28] When modern societies incorporate the variables of speed, complexity and interconnectedness, political order starts to disintegrate. In *Blade Runner*, even individual identity is ultimately subject to the profit considerations of multinational companies. Atherton asks whether this is fundamentally different from the world created by the virus, a world where hospitals and states across America were at some point in open bidding wars—using black market profiteers—for a finite supply of protective equipment. Senator Chris Murphy, a Democrat from Connecticut, wrote in an op-ed published on March 31, 2020, that the medical supply system had turned into "Lord of the Flies," the dystopian novel by British author William Golding. Replace the Tyrell Corporation in *Blade Runner* with Amazon and reframe the replicants as essential services, and suddenly you have a swarm of workers terrified that their jobs are a death sentence. Witness the transfiguration: a great human drama instead of a replicating virus. Things in America felt like a disaster movie. In Europe they just felt like a disaster.

Perhaps alone among all contemporary civilizations, America regards reality as an enemy to be defeated. That enemy takes many forms, but its essential nature remains unmodified. Those activists who traveled the coastal towns of Florida dressed as the Grim Reaper had a peculiar but nonetheless acute awareness of this. It was the image of death that they wanted to bring to the beautiful Florida beaches, as a warning to those who preferred to ignore the need to stay at home during a pandemic. Death is what is left of reality in our time: ineluctable and irrefutable, it alone continues to defy every technological fantasy.

The coronavirus is the purest instantiation of reality and in that sense the direst threat that a civilization built on its negation could expect to face. With a terrorist group one might refrain from any negotiation or dialogue, but its leaders can be threatened or deceived. The virus cannot be misled, bullied or cowed into submission. The day in March when he finally decided to take the threat seriously, Trump tweeted: "I am fully prepared to use the full power of the Federal Government to deal with our current challenge of the coronavirus!" It was the kind of ultimatum you might use against Iran or North Korea. It sounded less apt when directed against the coronavirus.

It was the wildest night. Sarah Palin rapping "Baby Got Back" on *The Masked Singer* straight into coverage of President Donald Trump speaking about a pandemic. Almost simultaneously, Tom Hanks announced that he and wife, Rita Wilson, were infected with the new coronavirus. Hanks, "America's Dad," perhaps the most loved man in the country and now part of an at-risk age group, would have been the choice of every scriptwriter for the role of famous victim, were this a disaster movie rather than real life.

At that moment, the question was sharply posed. Would Americans be brought back to reality by the seriousness of the threat? Or would they use it as an opportunity to leave reality behind, once and for all?

In one scenario, America might become more like the rest of the planet. The coronavirus crisis could prick the bubble of partisan discourse and help the country come together to create a universal healthcare system and deal with other pressing social issues such as gun control or homelessness. Even climate change might appear in a different light now that the American public had learnt to fear previously ignored threats to its collective safety.

The problem with this scenario is that the Covid crisis has moved the goalposts for social progress. Before the pandemic, progressives such as Bernie Sanders wanted the United States to adopt some of the policies prevalent in Western Europe. Now they are contemplating a revolution—and not of the kind that Sanders talked about. Free and universal healthcare. A reform of the prison system abolishing overcrowded and unsanitary facilities. A large shift of economic power towards workers, so that none are forced to risk their health in order to make a living. A new and revamped transit system that can no longer work as a vector of infection. Science education for all. Free and fast broadband. An end to the stigma of working from home. And so on. It seems implausible as a solution that Americans could ever adopt.

American society is exceptionally fragile. It lives in a state of permanent separation from reality. How do you address that? One could change the basic structure of society in order to make it more resilient, but the project would involve a form of social engineering: attention to detail and obedience to a single vision for social order. A second option would be to turn your back on the world and hope for the best. Sometimes that strategy works. It is bound to work for a while, simply as a result of the laws of probability. But the risks will grow and eventually reality strikes back. On December 7, 1941 and then again on September 11, 2001, the United States learned this lesson the hard way. On both occasions it was caught remarkably unprepared for events that, in their general form, were not that difficult to predict.

What was the response on both occasions? After the initial shock and recrimination, after the usual speeches rallying the country against the visible enemy—but the enemy had already become less visible the second time— a solution emerged that now seems logical and, from the point of view of American fortune, almost miraculous. The United States would not change the nature of its way of life because that would be equivalent to a form of surrender. But neither would it ever again allow itself to trust luck or fate against a hostile and dangerous world. Instead, it would build a barrier between the American dream and the real world, a security perimeter heavily monitored and guarded.

There are good reasons to believe that the same solution will be attempted in future wars against natural threats. There are reasons to believe it will be applied to climate change when its impact becomes far too evident and too costly to ignore. The irony is that a system of digital surveillance is already in place to deal with climate change. Without the constant monitoring and analysis of every realm of human activity, and without complex computer models to process the data, we would be blissfully unaware that climate change was even happening.

Contact tracing apps were not of much use during the current pandemic, but the questions they raised could not be more important. Should we take the first timid steps in developing a surveillance system that applies some of the lessons and expertise from counterterrorism and law enforcement to wider threats, such as pandemics? Much would depend on public perceptions, but these remain ambiguous. Activists and intellectuals firmly believe that the digital surveillance system put in place to prevent terrorist attacks is a profound threat to personal freedom; the general public is more sanguine.

I can detect three distinct stages in the way America has approached the pandemic; three distinct strategies or three kinds of escapism. The first stage was denial or oblivion. We have already seen how the country as a whole spent critical weeks dismissing the threat. The reasons for this are various, but they all come down to the fact that those who are busy creating imaginary worlds have no time or patience for the real one.

The strategy of oblivion was pursued to the limit, but by the first week of March 2020 it was becoming obvious that it could not be sustained. The human and economic costs were no longer a matter of opinion and, worse, it became possible to imagine a widespread collapse if nothing was done. At that point, a new strategy was silently envisaged. Americans would no longer ignore the virus. They would turn it into high drama. At some point during the summer of 2020, it became more important what to call the virus than to actually fight it.

The third way to escape from biological reality, the third stage of escapism, is also the most promising. The belief here is that any sufficiently advanced technology is indistinguishable from fantasy. Trump started as someone intent on ignoring the pandemic and he might end up being vindicated in his approach, with the crucial difference that this alternative reality will be a product of technological innovation rather than wishful thinking. It may even be possible that the pandemic was the necessary shock to get us to the singularity, the moment in technological development where humanity succeeds in eliminating the gravitational force of reality. By the end of 2020, with the arrival of miraculous new vaccine technologies, the third strategy of escapism started to pay off.

The use of Big Data and predictive algorithms has become a routine occurrence in counterterrorism and law enforcement. The chances that the system will be gradually expanded to include biosecurity look to be very high, not least because the coronavirus pandemic has already become immeasurably more devastating than any terrorist attack could hope to be. Ultimately, we need to bring the internet down to the physical world, to enhance our ability to understand physical processes in real time. And one needs to be able to act on that intelligence. The key will be the development of technologies to dramatically speed up the creation of new drugs and vaccines. With new exascale supercomputers, a billion times faster than our smartphones, it should be possible to run simulations of materials, including biochemical materials, in hours rather than days.[29] The El Capitan supercomputer should get to work at Lawrence Livermore National Laboratory in 2023. The nuclear weapons simulations it will perform are extraordinarily complex, modeling matter and energy shifting through temperatures ranging from room temperature to that at the center of the sun. Simulations must accommodate detail down to billionths of a meter for devices measuring meters in length. Soon one may be able to realistically model human biology as well and simulate interventions for diseases without the need for human trials, that is, by performing trials inside computer models. New vaccines could be developed in weeks.

Some scientists have called for the development of general vaccines targeting future viruses or entire virus families and creating prototype vaccines for all the most likely animal pathogens with pandemic potential ahead of time. Health organizations might then stockpile these types of vaccines in advance of the next potential pandemic.[30] It would be possible and maybe even desirable to conduct phase one and two human trials in advance of an outbreak. And what if a single vaccine could protect us not just from one specific virus but from the whole family of coronaviruses? That means many colds, SARS, Covid and thousands of other pathogens. Killer viruses we may not even know exist. According to Wayne Koff of the Human Vaccines Project, supercomputing and machine learning can eventually deliver a truly universal coronavirus vaccine: "If animal ecologists can gather enough data from the field, you create an algorithm to find the ones that have the greatest potential to jump species, and then the ones that would kill people."[31]

One year after the chaotic first few months, our evaluation of the American response is necessarily different. Americans acted as if the pandemic was not really taking place, but there was a hidden logic to it. Evading reality could be a working formula in the end, one achieved through revolutionary new vaccine technologies. Public policy measures, which doubtless saved many lives where they were effectively executed, could not by themselves get us to the world after Covid. What Vietnam or New Zealand were able to achieve was a way to reduce or eliminate the risk until the threat subsided, but not a way to end the threat. To return to my favorite image, those electing to introduce social restrictions as the main response to the pandemic were effectively suggesting that we should spend the rest of our existence inside a spacecraft, wandering in empty space, until our oxygen supply finally runs out—as it did in India in April 2021. With the vaccines, we were able to escape not only the virus but our response to the virus.

All this is new. Contrary to what people might think, vaccines and medicine more broadly played a relatively small role in fighting recent infectious diseases. We might expect measles deaths to have fallen only after the measles vaccine was introduced by John Enders and colleagues in 1963. Or scarlet fever, tuberculosis, typhoid and diphtheria. What happened in reality was that the vaccine solution has so far always come at the end, when casualties from all these diseases had already sharply dropped as a consequence of public health measures.[32] With Covid, remarkably, vaccines arrived so fast and they were so good that they became the primary force stopping the pandemic. In the United States and Europe, there is some cause to wonder whether it could ever be defeated without them, but by now it is possible to speak of a reversal of roles. If the first stage of the pandemic left the impression that the developed world was less able to deal with the threat, its final act looks dramatically different: while many developing countries struggle with the appearance of more contagious variants, Europe and North America can rely on their technological and financial might to deploy the most advanced vaccines. Many Asian economies, having escaped the pandemic with shallow downturns, now face challenges procuring and administering vaccines.

Covid left us with two main images of pandemic response. The Chinese success in containing the virus through social control and the American campaign to vaccinate its population at breakneck speed. The latter was driven by the desire to eliminate the biological threat rather than simply avoid it. In both cases, there was an element of control over nature, but only in the latter were human beings striving to emancipate themselves from the very natural forces they strove to master. Of course, vaccines are also a way to manipulate or even engineer human biology, but technological progress is never completed and thus the drive to master nature and escape its grip is never exhausted. Ultimately, human beings can only be safe from biological threats after they leave their biological nature behind. The religious meaning of every great plague in history took a technological turn this time.

The best technological prophets do not want to create a world where machines rule, where everything is predetermined and human beings are under surveillance by a vast system of control. The world to come is a world ruled by human beings endowed with supernatural powers, a magical world where many may even rise above human limitations, but the mind to govern human societies will be very different from an algorithm. Intuition, brilliance, genius: these qualities must be saved and, if saved, they can save the world. The world of the centaur—the combination of human and technological powers—is the world of myth, present in the Greek pantheon or the Vedas, where the superhuman power of the gods does not render them anonymous and abstract, but rather multiplies the wealth of their quarrels and quests.

In the Bhagavad Gita, Krishna tells Arjuna that as a warrior his duty is to fight, but the great warrior is not satisfied with power and victory. He tells Krishna that his mind is confused, that he needs to know the purpose of action. "Tell me surely this one thing: How should I attain the highest good?" And so he asks the god to draw up the chariot between the two armies on the battlefield, and they speak and argue as time stands still, the armies frozen in their place. As Sri Aurobindo puts it, the character of this inner crisis is not yet the questioning of the thinker. It is the sensational and moral revolt of the man hitherto satisfied with action but suddenly cast into a world of chaos, where the principles of action are in conflict with each other and there is no moral high ground left, "nothing to lay hold of and walk by, no *dharma*." Life as a battle and a field of death: the first law of this world is creation and preservation by destruction. "For this alone he takes refuge as a disciple with Krishna; give me, he practically asks, that which I have lost, a true law, a clear rule of action, a path by which I can confidently walk. He does not ask for the secret of life or of the world, the meaning and purpose of it all, but for a *dharma*."[33]

The pandemic has forced us to stop and think, while reminding us that, like Arjuna, our duty is indeed to fight and win. While the call to action can be answered through technology, the search for meaning is of a more spiritual nature. To become the masters and possessors of nature, as invulnerable as gods, it is first necessary to answer the question of what exactly is our nature and for what purpose should all this power be exercised. After all, the pandemic was a vivid reminder both of the threats contained within nature and of the inconvenient fact that we are part of nature, the natural carriers of the virus, one more segment in the infection chain and, therefore, not easily distinguishable from the threat. The modern movement of progress takes us in one direction, but there is a second and complementary path, a quieter one, leading to the discovery of the oldest truths about ourselves.

2

STAR WARS

The ancient Greek historian Thucydides was the first to write about the idea of great wars. There are many kinds of wars between states, fought for many reasons, and sometimes for no reason at all. The wars that shape history are those fought for the sake of the world order, such as the war between Athens and Sparta chronicled by Thucydides. There are wars, one could say, upon which the very fate of the world depends; what is at stake and what will be decided by the outcome is how world politics should be organized, according to which principles and values and, no less importantly, which hierarchy.

The pattern has been repeated many times throughout human history. A dominant state or empire, no matter how powerful, will be challenged by a new rising power, and, as the differential between them is reduced or disappears, the existing order becomes increasingly unstable. In almost all cases in history where a dominant power was ultimately replaced in the role, the change was determined by a momentous war. The exception, to which many books have been devoted, was the transition from British to American hegemony, and it can plausibly be explained by the cultural and historical links between the two countries. In other cases, of course, the challenger was defeated and the existing order survived. Just as Pax Britannica was giving way to Pax Americana, Imperial Germany saw its pretensions defeated on the battlefield. The fact that Britain came out of the war with its energies exhausted also helps explain what one scholar calls the "safe passage" to American hegemony.[1]

Every international system that the world has known has been a consequence of the profound realignments following such hegemonic struggles.[2] And, obviously, one might become convinced—especially after reading Thucydides—that wars for the world order will continue to take place for as long as humanity disagrees on how to organize itself. As Robert Gilpin puts it, wars have been functional and integral parts of the evolution and dynamics of international systems. It is difficult to see how the international system could change without great wars, tragic as the fact may be. Wars provide a radical upturn in the structure of prestige and authority and grant the victors a flawed but unambiguous mandate to reconstruct the world in their image. More directly, why would a hegemonic power peacefully give away its position at the apex of the system? Nor are there good examples of quickly rising powers that failed to press their advantage in a global conflict against rivals they saw as being in terminal decline.

The prospects for peaceful change at the level of the international system remain rather limited, but in the nuclear age change as such may also have to be ruled out. A war to define the very shape of global power would almost necessarily lead to the use of nuclear weapons, but a nuclear war would in turn lead to the destruction of the two contenders. To the extent that the model of hegemonic war needs to be revised today, the conclusion may be that change in the international system has become impossible. The authorities in Beijing have certainly been pondering this conundrum. How can China rise to the top if it can only hope to do that by dislodging a powerful incumbent, the country that created the existing system and has disproportionate access to its levers of power? To be sure, China was able to grow and expand while operating under that system, but there should be no illusions that it can continue to do so, even past the point where it would overtake the United States. As the last few years have already proved, Washington would never allow that to happen and, in a world with nuclear weapons, the path of open conflict is not possible either. Seen from Beijing, the situation would look like the eternal return of the same, with the possibility of diverting history in new directions irremediably closed. The cycle of growth and decline would have come to an end. In Washington, of course, the end would be applauded as the triumph of reason, the end time, the final judgment on the best way for humanity to organize itself.

We knew that a generalized race or competition between alternative geopolitical models had started, but it was never clear what the background for such a competition would be. If the clash took place within the existing global trade and financial system, which was of course built according to American rules and principles, the United States could be confident the battle could be decisively won. But what if it took place on neutral ground? What if it took place in a kind of neutral landscape, a state of nature with few or no rules, against a chaotic and quickly evolving background? The outcome would become considerably more uncertain.

The past few years have seemed to confirm much of what the theory of great wars would predict. Uneven growth in America and China had reduced the gap between the two countries, both in the economic and the military spheres. Political opinion in the United States suddenly woke up to the fact that China was a challenger to the existing international system. The country had become too powerful and too adept at technological innovation to rest satisfied with a subordinate role. In order to continue developing, China had to become much more assertive, and that helped convince Washington that a conflict with an unpredictable outcome might well become inevitable in the future.

For the time being, America still had the upper hand, but might it not be better to act now against Chinese power, rather than later when the tide would have turned in its favor? The international system was still in place. The United States had allies, unlimited access to the world's reserve currency, control over critical technologies such as semiconductors and a clear, if now shrinking, military advantage.

During the presidency of Donald Trump, these weapons were freely used, albeit in a haphazard manner. In Beijing they were received with growing apprehension, sometimes turning into gloom. By bringing a company such as Huawei to the brink of destruction, the United States had shown the true extent of its power, normally disguised by the routine operations of the international system. It had also made clear that China could not expect its companies to become global leaders; as a result, its economy seemed condemned to having a peripheral role in the world system. The existing hierarchy would not give way, nor could China hope to transform it from within. Conflict of an increasingly severe character now seemed inevitable.

The pandemic—emerging as the standoff over trade and technology reached a crescendo—provided a somewhat different answer to the question. The contemporary clash of civilizations, like similar clashes in the past, was never an intellectual war, a war of ideas. Ultimately the victors are those who master technology and acquire a higher level of control over natural forces. And the backdrop is not fixed or even stable. The battle will be fought over shifting sands as new threats emerge, as new technologies are developed and as changes in the global distribution of power erode the existing system.

The United States now faced a much more delicate and much more dangerous threat than those posed by Chinese manufacturing prowess or key digital technologies. Covid upset expectations and exposed weaknesses you might not know about. In a way, it forced America to compete with China on neutral ground, that of a new and unexpected technological and political threat to social stability.

There was always an argument that the existing world order cannot change, because only a momentous war has done that in the past and world wars have become impossible. But in pandemics and soon in climate change, we may have found two functional equivalents to war.

Addressing the opening of a study session at the Party School of the Chinese Communist Party in January 2021, a year after the first dramatic events in Wuhan, Xi Jinping noted the challenges resulting from the pandemic, supply chain disruptions and deteriorating relations with the West to conclude that "the world is in a turbulent time that is unprecedented in the past century." He sounded confident on what the year had meant for China. "Time and momentum are on our side. This is where we show our conviction and resilience as well as our determination and confidence."[3] As the virus spread to the whole world, it became apparent that Western societies did not have the ability to quickly organize every citizen around a single goal. As opposed to China, which remains to a large extent a revolutionary society, their political systems were built for normal times. Chinese society is a mobilized army, which can quickly drop everything else and march in one direction. As Mao once said, "Everything under heaven is in utter chaos, the situation is excellent." And so it seems at present, as seen from Beijing.

TRADE WARS REDUX

What started as a catastrophe for China is shaping up to be a moment of strategic opportunity, a rare turning point in the flow of history. Suddenly, the protests in Hong Kong, carrying a mortal threat to political stability in the mainland, became a physical impossibility. More importantly, the pandemic set in motion a global race to contain the virus for which China and the Chinese Communist Party seemed uniquely prepared. Whether the outcome was fully predictable or utterly surprising, "China ended the Year of Covid in many ways stronger than it started."[4] As the Chinese Communist Party approached its centenary in July 2021, the narrative of national rejuvenation reached a crescendo, with the pandemic serving as background for the rising arch of

Chinese power and pride. Rivalry with America was increasingly accepted and even celebrated. The meeting between top diplomats from the two countries in Alaska in March 2021 was a good symbol of Chinese confidence and brazenness, with Yang Jiechi assuming an imperious tone in which to berate and lecture his counterparts. The great trend of the moment was, as a popular formula among Party officials puts it, "a rising East and a declining West." In a speech in April 2021, Foreign Minister Wang Yi argued that democracy is not Coca-Cola, where the United States produces the original syrup and the whole world has one flavor. If there is only one model, one civilization on the planet, the world will lose its vitality and be devoid of growth.[5]

The increase in China's share of global gross domestic product (GDP) in 2020—by 1.1 percentage points—was the largest in a single year in many decades. The way China emerged from the pandemic more quickly than the United States is forcing economists to reconsider their predictions for the fateful moment when the Chinese economy overtakes its rival in size. The Japan Center for Economic Research previously expected the reversal to take place in 2036 or later. It now believes China could seize the crown of largest economy in the world as early as 2028. By then, we will likely have started to forget about Covid, but the two events will appear connected. The Centre for Economics and Business Research in London agrees with the forecast of 2028, albeit from a previous projection of 2033. As we will see below, the recovery in China helped attract a flood of capital, buoying up the yuan and increasing the size of the Chinese economy in dollar terms.

All these forecasts are of course highly contingent on developments in the United States. The early success of the vaccination campaign and a robust stimulus package approved in March 2021 could result in a real economic growth rate above 6%. In a note published in April and eloquently titled "Anatomy of a Boom," Goldman Sachs predicted more than 7% growth in 2021. By the end of the first quarter, a burst of growth left the American economy already within 1% of its peak in late 2019, before the pandemic hit, but fast growth has risks of its own, such as a sharp rise in consumer prices. The Federal Reserve expects inflation to rise above its target of 2% this year and to recede to that level by the end of 2022. The two rivals are not slowing down, and the question is who is growing in a more sustainable way.

In April 2020, China reported that its first-quarter GDP had contracted by 6.8% from the previous year, as the coronavirus outbreak seriously impacted the world's second largest economy, and authorities implemented large-scale shutdowns and quarantines to limit human contact. The recovery was just as quick. China's economy grew 2.3% in 2020, the only major economy to report positive growth in a pandemic-ravaged year.

By November, Chinese exports were growing by 21.1% from a year earlier, up from 11.4% in October. It was the highest growth rate since February 2018. As a result,

China's trade surplus surged to US$75.42 billion in November, up 102.9% from a year earlier, as export growth outstripped imports again. It was the largest trade surplus on record.[6] In December, exports grew 18.1% from a year earlier, with a trade surplus of US$78.2 billion. For the full year, the trade surplus reached US$535 billion, the highest since 2015.[7] China's export strength proved impervious to a rising Chinese yuan, which gained 6.1% against the dollar over the course of 2020.

While China had directed its stimulus packages to expanded credit for businesses and infrastructure, extraordinary fiscal support in developed economies channeled funds to households and consumers through transfers and income support. Remarkably, the pandemic seemed to exacerbate the imbalances in the global economy, with China acquiring an even greater role as the world's factory. Its own imbalances grew as well. Previous attempts to place the Chinese economy on a stabler path by shifting focus towards domestic consumers and away from exports were reversed. In 2020 Chinese exports surged, but spending per capita fell 4%. With the yuan continuing to rise against the dollar, some rebalancing towards consumption might still happen, creating pressure for Chinese exporters and making imports relatively cheaper.

The strong trade growth in 2020 came as other parts of the world grappled with severe coronavirus outbreaks, driving up demand for medical gear and lockdown goods made in China. Shipments of electronic goods surged to US$166 billion, a year-on-year increase of 24.81%. In November 2020, medical equipment exports soared 38%, plastic products 112% and lighting gear 47%, a record-breaking month for China's exporters. Chinese factories exported 224 billion masks from March through December, or almost 40 for every man, woman and child on the planet outside of China. The shipments were worth 340 billion yuan, which is about 2% of all Chinese exports in 2020.[8]

The biggest market for Chinese goods in November 2020 was, perhaps surprisingly, the United States, which bought US$51.9 billion worth, a year-on-year increase of 46%. In December, exports to the U.S. jumped 34.5%. For the full year, China's trade surplus with the U.S. reached another record of US$316.9 billion. China's relatively quick containment of the virus resulted in factories being up and running in time to produce the electronic goods, household appliances, furniture and medical supplies that the world needed as the virus fanned out across the planet. At Guangdong Xinbao Electrical Appliances, which makes household goods such as bread makers, blenders and coffee machines, the order book was full. European and American buyers now had to pay 80 to 100% up front to secure their goods.[9]

Strong demand for Chinese products from the United States ensured that shipping costs reached all-time highs. At the Port of Los Angeles, the country's largest processor of container cargo and the gateway for many Chinese goods, shipping containers carrying Chinese imports were, as the *New York Times* put it, "stacked like Legos in piles six high." October 2020 was the busiest month in the port's long history, and traffic has remained high. The volume of containers handled at the California ports of Los Angeles and Long Beach grew 45% in February 2021 compared with a year earlier, climbing for an eighth consecutive month. In March, container volume at the Port of Los Angeles surged by more than 80%.[10]

The surge, not matched by corresponding Chinese imports of American goods, created an interesting problem: finding containers into which all those goods could fit. China's exports were so strong that far more shipping containers were leaving Chinese ports than were coming back.[11] Containers have never been so sought after. In early November, the eight major shipping hubs, including Shanghai and Ningbo, saw container throughput rising by 13.1% year on year, according to data from the China Ports and Harbors Association. Container manufacturers were working twenty-four hours a day and seven days a week to meet the demand.[12] By December, workers at the Port of Los Angeles were plucking containers of toys off ships and out of massive stacks of cargo swamping docks at the Southern California trade gateway to get holiday gifts under trees in time for Christmas. With so much cargo flooding in ahead of Christmas, the port was "essentially in a triage situation."[13]

China benefited from its broad manufacturing production base, and lockdown goods such as laptops and home appliances had by and large been excluded from the tariffs approved by the Trump administration over the previous two years. But the numbers also revealed the greatest swing in transpacific imbalances since the global financial crisis. As Brad Setser commented, one had to wonder whether it would be politically sustainable for the economic stimulus in the United States to do more to support Chinese production than production at home.[14] As one of the only economies growing during the pandemic, and a giant one at that, China should have been providing a lift to others by hoovering up their products. Instead, it was riding on stimulus policies elsewhere. China's largest monthly trade surplus on record required a deficit for the rest of the world of nearly 1.2% of GDP, the equivalent of a substantial fiscal contraction. In April 2021, the U.S. Department of the Treasury, in one of its reports, called for China to implement forceful measures to boost domestic demand: "China should take decisive steps to allow for greater market openness by implementing structural reforms to reduce state intervention, enhancing social safety nets and increasing spending on healthcare and unemployment benefits, and permitting a greater role for market forces."[15] Brad Setser has in the meantime been appointed Counselor to the United States Trade Representative.

When Congress passed its third Covid relief bill in February 2021, the first under the Biden administration, one had to wonder if the spending measures would not in fact provide a boost to Chinese manufacturers. Congress had passed a US$900 billion relief program in December, and the package approved at the beginning of the pandemic was about US$2 trillion. What Biden was proposing was a new US$1.9 trillion program that would send out US$1,400 per person under certain income levels, extend emergency unemployment insurance programs, help schools and localities survive the impact of the lockdowns and extend paid leave. As former Treasury Secretary Larry Summers was quick to note, the proposal committed 15% of GDP with essentially no increase in public investment. After resolving the coronavirus crisis, how would political and economic space be found for public investments in such critical areas as infrastructure, education or renewable energy?[16] About US$360 billion of the new stimulus package will be spent on imports, with Chinese exports likely to increase by US$60 billion over 2021 and 2022. The package could increase China's GDP by 0.5% over the next year. The export boost would give businesses room to spend on expanding capacity, allowing China to maintain its high levels of investment even as state spending on infrastructure slows, according to UBS chief China economist Wang Tao.[17]

In April 2021, when Biden announced his US$2.3 trillion American Jobs Plan, better known as the infrastructure bill, the level of ambition seemed markedly smaller. The spending, at least half of which has little to do with infrastructure, will be spread out over eight years, which means it will add less than US$300 billion a year in federal investments.[18] The plan will be partly funded by corporate tax increases, with Janet Yellen urging Congress to offset the cost of the new investment plans in order to contain the deficit. "We don't want to use up all of that fiscal space and over the long run, deficits need to be contained to keep our federal finances on a sustainable basis. So, I believe that we should pay for these historic investments," she said.[19] For critics, the tax hike could once again induce American companies to expand overseas. Commentators also noted that China loomed large in the new policies. The global competition for primacy is now shaping American economic policy at home. This is how Biden first introduced his American Jobs Plan, a speech where he mentioned China six times: "It will grow the economy, make us more competitive around the world, promote our national security interests, and put us in a position to win the global competition with China in the upcoming years."

As for China's economic presence in Europe, 2020 was a genuinely historic year: for the first time, China became the European Union's main trade partner, taking the top spot previously occupied by the United States. Exports of European goods to China increased by 2.2%

and imports went up 5.6%, impressive figures for a year when the pandemic severely impacted transatlantic trade, with the EU exporting 8.2% less to the United States and imports falling by 13.2%. I have written in a previous book about the growing integration between Asia and Europe and the changes that the "dawn of Eurasia" bring to the world order.[20] The pandemic made the process quicker and more evident.

As a result of Covid-19, global foreign direct investment in the first half of 2020 declined by the largest amount on record. Inflows into the United States, usually the largest recipient, were down 61%; inflows into the European Union were off by 29%. In contrast, inflows into China were down only 4%, and monthly inflows have strengthened since. In the third quarter of 2020, inflows expanded nearly 17% compared with the same period in 2019.[21] China actually ended the year with a small increase of 4%. In the United States the final figure was a decrease of 49%. China became the largest recipient of global foreign direct investment, attracting an estimated US$163 billion in inflows, followed by the United States with US$134 billion. For the first time ever, the roles were reversed. The European Union, in the meantime, saw inflows drop by 71% to an estimated US$110 billion.

If the pandemic and its aftershocks continue to impact the production capacity in India and other major economies, there will be a considerable flow of orders coming to Chinese manufacturing, accelerating expansion plans. The container shortage described above has its equivalent in shortages of labor in Chinese manufacturing, so companies are having to step up investment in robotics. The *South China Morning Post* reported that:

> In 2018, the number of newly installed industrial robots in China fell 1 per cent, to around 154,000 units. The market continued to shrink in 2019, dropping 8.6 per cent from a year earlier to 144,000 units, according to figures from China Robot Industry Alliance and the International Federation of Robotics. But there was a sharp rebound in the latter part of 2020.[22]

Robotics has also become more popular as a result of the lockdowns and their impact on worker mobility. According to Luo Jun of the International Robotics and Intelligent Equipment Industry Alliance, China's goal is to reduce the dependency on imports of core robotics parts, and that could be expedited "if global demand remains strong and continues to rely on Chinese production capacity." The impact of the pandemic on the global industrial supply chain has been a major stimulus, forcing a huge number of orders to return to China.

Early in the pandemic, the Chinese authorities unveiled a fiscal stimulus package of nearly 3.6 trillion yuan, including an increase of the budget fiscal deficit to a record high of 3.6% of GDP, up from 2.8% the year before. It was the first time the ratio exceeded 3%, a red line for decades. The package added 1 trillion yuan to the budget. Another trillion yuan came from special treasury bonds, though these will not be included in the central government budget and therefore the deficit ratio. The local government special bond quota, a source of infrastructure funding, was boosted by 1.6 trillion yuan.

By both historical and global standards, it was a modest expansion. By the end of 2020, the Covid response in the U.S. had seen a US$12,800 increase in debt per capita; in the United Kingdom the figure was US$7,000 and in Germany and France, US$5,300. In China, it was a mere US$1,200. The Western world responded with massive increases in budget deficits, which could constrain future policy options, while China did not.[23] A relatively quick recovery from the pandemic, without a major fiscal stimulus, allowed China to maintain higher interest rates and a stronger currency. Despite several cuts to key policy rates, the yield-to-maturity of Chinese central government bonds stayed well above that of their U.S. peers. In the universe of corporate bonds, Chinese credit offers more attractive yields than its counterparts in developed markets. This is attracting large investment inflows to Chinese securities.[24] Investors such as Ray Dalio now see the need to have "a significant portion" of their portfolio in Chinese assets for long-term diversification and shorter-term tactical trading purposes.[25]

Foreign inflows to Chinese bonds reached an all-time high in the second quarter of 2020 at US$33.5 billion.

Foreign holdings of Chinese government debt through the market link in Hong Kong grew by more than 900 billion yuan in the first eleven months of 2020. In November, the Shanghai Stock Exchange slammed the brakes on Ant Group's initial public offering, set to be the biggest stock debut in history with investors on multiple continents and at least US$34 billion in proceeds, but even then the bourse continued on track to rank the first in the world for initial public offerings in the year that marked its thirtieth anniversary. Louis-Vincent Gave noted: "Just as water flows downhill, capital tends to flow to where it is best rewarded."[26] During the first year of the pandemic, investors certainly bought more Chinese government bonds, with their ownership share of the market increasing to account for about 9% of the market.

In the United States, interest rates are at historic lows, but the political will to raise rates is no longer present because it would have such a devastating impact on bond markets and the real economy. At present, with the Federal Reserve still buying US$120 billion of bonds a month, even modest rises in yields will be swamped by relentless purchases by central banks. The question is whether investors will continue to flow to the dollar if the currency can no longer generate yield. But in that case, where will the money come from to buy these bonds and fund these deficits across the board?

In an article published in January 2021, the former member of the Federal Reserve Board Kevin Warsh warned that, while China might not be ready yet to challenge the dollar directly, it had its sights on the bond markets and was taking steps to displace Treasury notes and bonds as the world's most important safe asset. "The clear and concerted message to global investors: Invest in China and get better, safer returns."[27] Ominously, the vulnerability of the Treasury market became clearer when Covid fears struck in March 2020. Foreign holders sold, net of purchases, a record amount of almost US$300 billion Treasury bonds and bills. About one-fifth of these sales were by foreign official institutions, including central banks.[28] Prices fell unexpectedly, even as equity prices plummeted. Yields spiked 0.75%, one of the largest, fastest shifts in years. Furthermore, although the dollar did appreciate in March 2020, which is consistent with flight to safety during market turbulence, the degree of appreciation in the dollar against other currencies was much smaller than that during the Global Financial Crisis. If Treasury securities no longer provide the safe haven that investors seek, they will have to find alternative investment strategies to fill that role. Whether the March meltdown was an omen of deeper realignments is still an open question. Everyone agrees that, based on past experience, the episode should never have happened.

THE STATE OF NATURE AS A STATE OF WAR

Relatively common as it has become, the notion that China has been better than Western societies at fighting

Covid suffers from one major problem: China is not playing the same game. While European countries or the United States regarded the pandemic as a public health problem, for the Chinese authorities it was always a national security crisis. It involved questions of existential importance: the international stature of China, the viability of its national plans and perhaps even the final survival of the regime. When the instructions from Beijing arrived in January 2020, Wuhan's public health authorities said they were in a "state of war" against the virus as they attempted to quarantine the city to curb its spread. A committee of Wuhan's top officials said the city must "strictly implement emergency response requirements, enter into a state of war, and implement wartime measures to resolutely curb the spread of this epidemic." They added, "Homes must be segregated, neighbors must be watched." Months later, when the situation started to normalize, authorities began to speak of a mere "state of emergency."

Perhaps those authorities had no alternative. After all, many commentators in the United States reacted to news of the outbreak in Wuhan by describing it as a national security crisis for Beijing. A *Financial Times* correspondent famously argued that the Chinese regime was now approaching one of those moments, recurrent in Chinese history, when the rulers lost the mandate of heaven and were overthrown. Covid could "turn out to be China's Chernobyl moment, when the lies and absurdities of autocracy are laid bare for all to see."[29] The feeling was echoed by the American National Security Advisor at the time, Robert O'Brien. One Australian former diplomat and intelligence official argued in February 2020 that the virus outbreak would make it harder for Xi Jinping to sustain the mix of internal obedience and global respect required for China's bid to dominate the region: Australia should take advantage of the opportunity.[30] In the end, as a country in the middle of a swift ascent in the global power ranking, and the country where the pandemic originated, the stakes would always be much higher in China than elsewhere.

Since the outbreak was regarded as an imminent threat to the status of the country and the survival of the regime, the measures adopted were drastic and absolute. Everything else took second stage. A swift victory was the only scenario contemplated and the tools were commensurate to the task. The government white paper on the pandemic, issued on June 7, 2020, portrayed the process as a grand battle—a people's war (人民战争) under Xi Jinping's personal command (亲自指挥)—that showcased the strength and advantages of the Chinese political system.[31]

China did beat Covid, but remember that it was not playing by the same rules as Europe or the United States, and therefore any comparison between the outcomes must be subtler than many assume. It is because China was playing by a different set of rules that a clash of perceptions became inevitable. Chinese diplomacy has paid a heavy price as a result. Not diplomatic clumsiness but the opposition of intellectual frameworks explains why China's image has suffered from what—on a different dimension—has to be described as an effective response to the pandemic. In Europe, that opposition took on dramatic overtones: Europeans regarded Covid as a global health crisis, where cooperation across borders had a role to play, and were shocked to discover that the Chinese authorities saw it as a unique occasion for intense global competition. In January and February 2020, foreign governments were asked to send medical equipment to China and to avoid making that aid public. When those countries sought masks and ventilators from Chinese companies, they discovered the price included public praise for China and even the ruling regime.[32]

Perceptions of China in Europe and elsewhere took a negative turn. A survey from the Pew Research Center, published in October 2020, showed that a majority in each of the surveyed countries had an unfavorable opinion of China. In Australia, the United Kingdom, Germany, the Netherlands, Sweden, the United States, South Korea, Spain and Canada, negative views reached their highest points since the Center began polling on the topic more than a decade ago. Did those facts have political consequences? By the end of 2020, the European Union announced it would be signing an investment agreement with China aimed at bringing the two economies closer together. Among European governments, easier access to the Chinese market was regarded as part of the recovery, but rising diplomatic tensions between the two sides, including the imposition of individual sanctions by both Brussels and Beijing, rendered a swift ratification of the agreement increasingly unlikely.

In the state of exception created by the virus, the power of real life broke through the protective glass of the international order. Many in China saw it as a moment of liberation, with the nationalist commentator Li Yi openly celebrating at a forum in Shenzhen that China could now beat the United States in a fair game: the virus game.[33] But suppose commentators such as Li are correct? Were the great rivalry between China and the United States to proceed outside the constraints of existing rules and practices, China would lose many benefits it enjoyed under that framework. Great power rivalry would then take a new form, with the main powers competing to determine who might be better prepared to create a new system from a chaotic state of nature. It is not clear that China would win. At the very least, such a contest would remove all illusions, still common in Washington, that a contest for the world order could be avoided. Donald Trump showed that once freed from its usual shackles, American power can be overwhelming. After all, while China was relatively better at fighting the virus, the pandemic also showed its weakness at what the Communist Party calls ideological struggle. Every misstep was mercilessly explored by its ideological opponents, whose access to the global media landscape far exceeds the resources of the Party. It is doubtful that the regime has gained in prestige. When the gloves come off, Washington seems to acquire some tangible advantages.

The international system has changed rather dramatically since Joe Biden perfected his foreign policy ideas. As the Chinese authorities now like to repeat, we live in the age of a great realignment. Bigger changes are afoot than humanity has seen in hundreds of years. This world is not conducive to multilateralism and cooperation. In a revolutionary period, your priority is to spot the chances to get ahead and turn events in your favor. The main problem for Biden will be how to reconcile these new facts with his strong desire to return to a simpler world. He is attracted to the finished product—a global liberal order governed from Washington—but seems uninterested in the geopolitical processes that necessarily precede it.

As Jake Sullivan and Kurt Campbell put it in an essay published two years ago, the new policy will marshal the soft coercion of the global order: "If China hopes to enjoy equal access to this new economic community, its own economic and regulatory frameworks must meet the same standards."[34] The global order has a certain gravitational pull, forcing China to choose between following its rules or willingly become an outcast. Similarly, its growing technological clout will require some enhanced restrictions on the flow of technology investment and trade in both directions, but these efforts should be carefully targeted to prevent permanent damage to the global liberal order. "Failing to do so," Sullivan and Campbell write, "could Balkanize the global technology ecosystem by impeding flows of knowledge and talent." Since being chosen by Biden for the role of National Security Advisor, Sullivan has been following and implementing these basic intuitions.

Even though the "global liberal order" is often a tool used to project American power, it also imposes some constraints on the United States. An outright ban on certain Chinese companies, for instance, might be regarded as incompatible with the upholding of global rules and principles. One obvious example was the threat of an imminent shutdown that the Trump administration used as a way to force the sale of Chinese tech company TikTok to a group including Oracle. The Biden administration decided not to enforce the order, with the process "being led by officials who have sometimes been critical of Mr. Trump's targeting of Chinese tech companies, although they have expressed a range of views on how to respond to the complex challenge."[35]

Similarly, forms of economic coercion against allies might be excluded, but without them the United States might not be able to force those allies to reduce their economic links with China. Trump did not prima facie exclude any method or tactic, because the contest did not take place under a normative order. His administration faced a different problem: once you removed the rules and values projected by the existing international order, the United States had to operate in a void. What goals were the Trump administration pursuing? Released from the regulative idea of a world order to whose promotion the country had been committed, Washington was free to do anything, or almost anything. It felt lost. In practice, this meant that the policy towards China, rather bellicose in spirit, was taken over by a chaotic combination of goals coming from different officials and departments, or then a rather arbitrary and meaningless objective such as reducing the trade deficit, which the phase one trade agreement Trump agreed with China in late 2019 failed to deliver.

In a second essay, this time coauthored with Hal Brands, Sullivan returns to the notion of the global order as the arena where the contest between China and the United States will be decided. Sullivan and Brands are less worried that the United States might have left its flank in the Pacific vulnerable, than with the possibility that China could leap directly to the role of managing and leading the global order. Its efforts came at a time when the United States, during the Trump administration, stepped back from its traditional role as guarantor of the international order. Whoever occupies that role has the critical advantage. But the crucial point is that, according to the authors, China is not tailored for the role: "China may well be less capable of providing global public goods than the United States, both because it is less powerful and because its authoritarian political system makes it harder to exercise the comparatively enlightened, positive-sum leadership that has distinguished U.S. primacy."[36]

Biden will try to use the "global liberal order" against China. Trump always favored a direct clash, one taking place in a fundamentally chaotic or disordered world. For Biden, world politics still follows an organized set of values and rules. China will be asked to at least pay formal tribute to that order, or else be sanctioned in accordance with the rules. Trump, of course, never cared much about rules. He saw them less as a tool than as an obstacle.

As Trump advisors H. R. McMaster and Gary D. Cohn put it in a notable *Wall Street Journal* article in 2017, Trump embarked on his presidency with a revolutionary new outlook that saw the world not as a "global community" governed by rules and institutions, "but an arena where nations, nongovernmental actors and businesses engage and compete for advantage." The story of this article remains somewhat mysterious. On the one hand, it is a chilling prophecy of a new kind of world order or, more properly, world disorder. On the other, it was signed by two conventional thinkers, so conventional that they soon departed from the turmoil of the Trump administration. And yet it was from them that we heard an unprecedented call for the geopolitics of the "arena." They added: "Rather than deny this elemental nature of international affairs, we embrace it."[37]

In an ideal world, China would be subject to genuinely global norms. The question is what the enforcement mechanisms are. Do the United States and its allies still have the ability to bring about the necessary level of compliance with liberal norms? Indeed, the limits to American power have only grown since the Iraq invasion—the Global Financial Crisis, the chaos of the Trump presidency and the current pandemic continued the process—and seem increasingly connected to the worldwide diffusion of technological power and the growth of rival economic blocs and ideological models. The age of global empires—even a liberal one—may turn out to have been strictly confined in time, dependent on imbalances of technology and knowledge of an inexorably transitory character.

As much as the Biden presidency represents a return to the past, it is easy to see that the world has changed beyond recognition. The state of exception threatens to become more or less permanent. In March 2019, a professor of economics at Tsinghua University in Beijing argued that China could curb its exports of pharmaceuticals to the United States as a countermeasure in the ongoing trade wars. Li Daokui delivered the veiled threat at a general meeting of the Political Consultative Conference, a political advisory group, as part of the annual National People's Congress. "Indeed we are at the mercy of others when it comes to computer chips, but we are the world's largest exporter of raw materials for vitamins and antibiotics," he said. "Should we reduce the exports, the medical systems of some Western countries will not run well."[38]

After Covid, the episode acquired a deeper resonance. Suddenly the United States found itself facing shortages of medical supplies and equipment, much of them manufactured in China. Biden started speaking about the need to eliminate supply chain vulnerabilities across a range of critical products for which Americans were dangerously dependent on foreign suppliers: not just medical supplies or pharmaceuticals, but energy technology, semiconductors, telecommunications infrastructure and key raw materials such as rare earths. A plan published in July 2020, during the height of the summer infection wave, affirmed the need to ensure that America would never again face a shortage of vital goods, while stressing that those vital goods may be different in the future, particularly during a future crisis. Therefore, a plan to rebuild supply chains extends potentially to every sector and every product and must be institutionalized in a permanent process.[39]

In February 2021, the White House said it was identifying potential chokepoints in the semiconductor supply

chain after coming under pressure from car manufacturers facing a global shortage. General Motors halted production in its Kansas, Canada and Mexico plants. The
shortage was exacerbated by the sanctions against
Chinese chipmakers implemented during the Trump
administration, a vivid example of how trade wars are
much more complex games than they look at first. What
could the Biden administration do? Sacrifice the economic recovery to the old rules and principles governing
global markets? According to those principles, semiconductors should be used by those industries with greater
profit margins and produced in those countries with a
competitive advantage in the sector. Instead, the crisis
fueled calls for the reshoring of semiconductor manufacturing on national security grounds, and the chief executives of Intel and Qualcomm, among others, wrote to the
president to warn that without further support, the
country's "technology leadership is at risk."[40] In March
2021, Intel announced it would be entering the contract
chipmaking business, and would woo customers such as
Apple and Qualcomm, which until now have relied on
Taiwan Semiconductor Manufacturing. The company
will be spending roughly US$20 billion to build two chip
facilities in Arizona. It will surely have government backing for the project, which was immediately praised by
U.S. Secretary of Commerce Gina Raimondo.[41]

In a recent report to Congress, the Pentagon blamed
Wall Street and "a radical vision of free trade" for under-

mining the defense base. It noted that, while microelectronics are present in the most complex weapons the Department of Defense buys—including nuclear weapons—today only 12% of all microchips produced worldwide come out of the American companies that gave Silicon Valley its name. "China is projected to dominate global semiconductor production by 2030, and in the meantime, current suppliers in Taiwan, South Korea, Malaysia, and elsewhere are in easy range of Chinese missiles, subversion, or air or maritime interference." The conclusion is that Beijing is already in a position to threaten or disrupt the entire American defense supply chain, rendering the pandemic shortages minuscule by comparison.[42] "It is the rise of China, above all else, that is bringing nationalistic management of the economy back into the political mainstream."[43]

In her hearing before the Senate Finance Committee on February 25, the new U.S. Trade Representative Katherine Tai was asked whether the goal of a trade agreement between two modern, developed economies should be the elimination of tariffs and trade barriers. She declined to agree. "Maybe if you had asked me this question five or ten years ago, I would have been inclined to say yes," Tai responded.[44] She added that she shared the Trump administration's goal of bringing supply chains back to America, but that its policies had created "a lot of disruption and consternation." Tactics, not the goals, were the problem. Suddenly, to regard trade through the lens of multilateral institutions looks irremediably naive.

Some commentators have defended the establishment of "mutual defense trade pacts triggering automatic tariffs against China to protect American allies such as Australia or Norway from Chinese economic coercion." The model, of course, is the system of alliances operating in the security area. A member of the alliance of democracies subjected to economic coercion by an autocracy could invoke an article of mutual protection to summon the unified support of fellow democracies. "Beyond the economic impact, the symbolism of such solidarity would be a potent deterrent. Bullies respond to strength and exploit weakness. A coordinated response would make them think twice before acting."[45]

The iron logic of the process is to have two separate supply chains, one for the Chinese market and one for much of the rest of the world, rather than a single network governed by common rules. Foxconn, the mammoth Taiwanese company, now says it expects manufacturing to fragment into different production networks.[46] But these separate networks inhabit the same external environment. They still fight for suppliers and markets and try to keep one step ahead of their rivals. If the Chinese dream is to be able to compete outside the existing order, that dream may be very close to realization.

DUAL CIRCULATION

Take the case of the automobile industry in China. The prevalence of joint ventures indicates a unique developmental model, in which foreign and Chinese automakers cooperate in building highly efficient value chains. Joint ventures are legal partnerships between a domestic firm and a foreign investor to form a new operation in the domestic market, and typically involve widespread use of proprietary technologies, intellectual property and advanced production methods. This model was extremely successful in China, less so elsewhere. To gain a foothold in an overseas market, international automakers generally prefer direct exports, or to set up wholly owned corporations. The establishment of joint ventures has often been a compromise for the foreign firms and indicates strong negotiating power on the part of the host country, which sees it as a way to force some measure of technology transfer.

China deliberately avoided both the Mexican and the Korean models of subordination to large foreign firms or autonomous national development respectively, opting to integrate its automobile industry in global value chains while preserving control over the process. In China, enterprises owned by the central government all set up international joint ventures, while national carmakers are all private companies.

This example is a good way to understand the logic behind the "dual circulation" (双循环) strategy introduced by Xi Jinping in the May 2020 Politburo meeting.[47] The strategy is a major theoretical innovation deserving much closer study in the West than it has received so far. It is also acutely attuned to the new external conditions introduced by the pandemic, even if it was developed in advance. Formally, it introduces a clear break between a domestic and a global economic system: the two circulations. Something of the concept had been present in Chinese practice. As we have seen, control in the auto sector is drastically different depending on whether a company is operating in the national or the global system, and the difference followed the intuition that a company needs the backing of the Chinese state when dealing with foreign interests or counterparts. Now, after the trade wars and after the pandemic, that intuition is being transformed into a new general concept meant to guide Chinese economic policy as a whole. Deng Xiaoping, by contrast, had spoken of a "great international circulation" (国际大循环) strategy. In 1987, Wang Jian, an economic official in the State Planning Commission, proposed the "Theory of Grand International Circulation," gleefully supported by the leadership of Deng Xiaoping and Zhao Ziyang. The proposal advocated moving agricultural laborers to heavy industries, following the model of Taiwan and South Korea, and shifting China's economy towards exports. It was the beginning of the Chinese economic miracle.

The new "dual circulation" strategy is not a strategy of economic autarchy. The signing of the Regional Comprehensive Economic Partnership by China and fourteen negotiating partners on November 15, 2020 is testimony to China's continued international outlook. What the strategy argues is that the "two economies" must follow different rules. The domestic system is governed by a general imperative of efficiency, which is often pursued through competition between private actors. In the global system, however, efficiency is a subordinate goal. State power, national security and national greatness are much more important. While supply chains in the domestic system may be left to the outcomes of the market, abroad they must be built and protected through the use of state power and state resources. In other words, a "dual circulation" strategy is actually a strategy of economic globalization. What Xi is saying is that Chinese economic expansion will not be left to international rules or the vagaries of global markets.

In other words, the global arena is one with very few rules, and successful states need to rely on a fully developed domestic economy to increase their ability to compete globally. The worst outcome for a country is to find itself in a position of dependency. This dependency is particularly visible today in some core technologies, suggesting that China should improve its independent capacity to innovate. The best outcome is to use the energies and efficiency of its domestic circulation in order to increase leverage over other states.

As argued above, "dual circulation" is not only the first major contemporary Chinese contribution to economic thought. It is also an extraordinarily appealing and powerful idea for a world turned upside down by the pandemic. Many of the tentative steps being taken by the Biden administration could be described as examples of the core concepts advanced by "dual circulation." What the European Union calls "open strategic autonomy" in trade and technology shares some of its elements. China is getting ready for the worst in a world that every day gives signs that the worst is part of the possible: disruption of supply chains, closure of borders, trade wars, cutthroat competition for scarce resources. "Dual circulation" is a response to the crumbling or dissolution of the international order.

In an intriguing speech given in April 2020, but not publicized before November—the first lengthy treatment of dual circulation—Xi Jinping openly starts with the pandemic: "The world today is going through changes seen once in a century, and this pandemic is also something encountered once in a century. It is both a crisis and a major test." Later he adds: "The current pandemic is a stress test under actual combat conditions." Xi refers to the old "great international circulation" (国际大循环) strategy, pointing out that it is starting to encounter headwinds, which may be intensified by the pandemic. An advantage of a country as large as China is that an "internal circulation" is possible. Importantly, however, he links the expansion in the domestic economy to continued "opening up," pointing out that the stronger the former becomes, the "greater the gravitational force it exerts on global resource factors" and—this is of critical importance—the more it facilitates the formation of new advantages when participating in international competition and cooperation. The pandemic has exposed risks in the global supply chain. In order to safeguard its industrial and national security, China "must focus on building production chains and supply chains that are independently controllable, secure and reliable, and strive for important products and supply channels to all have one alternative source, forming the necessary industrial backup system." The conclusion is both logical and sobering: the final goal is to "increase international dependence on China, forming powerful countermeasures and deterrent capabilities against foreign parties."[48]

It is not surprising, then, that Chinese commentators draw a direct connection between the pandemic and "dual circulation." The current world political and economic situation is so turbulent that China cannot take anything for granted: even if it overcame the immediate impact from the pandemic at home, the Chinese economy had to deal with a demand shock coming from outside and repeated disruptions in industrial and supply chains. The supply chain layout will face dramatic adjustment possibilities, with all current positions being challenged. As a result, according to Huang Qunhui, China must shift from a passive to an active policy. It is in a good position do so because of the breadth of its industrial base, the most diversified in the world, and the size of its domestic market. In an increasingly turbulent world, China could do better than its direct competitors.[49] But if domestic strength dominates, that does not mean one should not attach importance to the international economic cycle. In fact, in times of global turmoil one main error must be avoided at all costs: a retreat from the global economy and the irreparable loss of international influence. The new development pattern of "double circulation" that the Chinese authorities aim to achieve will actually expand that influence, and make China the center of a new international division of labor, the explicit aim of its long-term geopolitical initiative, the Belt and Road. As Huang and others put it, the goal is to make foreign industry more dependent on China's supply chain and China's huge consumer market.

What is the Belt and Road? As I argue in a previous book, the best way to answer this question is to directly address what the Belt and Road is for.[50] As China continues to rise to the pinnacle of the world economy, it faces increasing difficulties and resistance. Part of these difficulties are political, and the Belt and Road does in fact anticipate their development. In some respects, the initiative helped crystallize a more antagonistic position towards China in the United States and India, but those developments were inevitable, and the Belt and Road tried to address them in advance by putting in place the rudiments of a Chinese-led global economic network.

The difficulties are also economic, and perhaps primarily so. It is common in liberal circles to believe that a country can move up the technological value chain by focusing on domestic reforms and policies. The Chinese authorities do not take this approach seriously. They believe in the existence of a global political order. Countries occupy different positions in the existing order. If a country as large as China wants to move closer to the center, it can only hope to do so by operating a series of changes akin to a worldwide revolution. That is the fundamental meaning of the Belt and Road.

In order to become a technological leader, China needs to vastly expand its global presence and influence. There are three main reasons why this is the case. First, the investment in new key technologies is so massive that it can only have an adequate return if access to genuinely global markets is assured. But how can they be assured if powerful competitors will do everything to close them off to Chinese companies? Second, you need access to global value chains and reliable suppliers. If a country wants to move its factors of production to higher segments of the value chain, it needs to ensure a reliable network of suppliers. Third, it needs to transform its own key technologies into global standards—the source of endless streams of revenue in royalties and licensing fees—a process highly dependent on its ability to exercise power within the international bodies responsible for determining what these global standards are.

Chinese officials lead at least four global standards organizations, including the International Telecommunication Union, a United Nations body governing phone and internet connectivity, and the International Electrotechnical Commission, an industry group governing electrical and electronic technologies. Chinese executives and officials have a saying, one I heard often during my time living in Beijing: third tier companies make products. Second tier companies make technology. Top tier companies set standards.[51]

Leadership in standards is not a novel concept, of course. Werner von Siemens, the German industrialist and founder of the famous conglomerate carrying his name, noted in his memoirs, published shortly after his death in 1892:

> A main reason of the rapid growth of our factories is, in my opinion, that the products of our manufacture were in large part results of our own inventions. Though these were in most cases not protected by patents, yet they always gave us the start on our competitors, which usually lasted until we gained a fresh start by new improvements.[52]

Needless to say, the pandemic simultaneously created a number of difficulties for the Belt and Road initiative. They were first of all logistical. Several projects in South and Southeast Asia had to be put on hold after the virus forced Chinese workers and engineers to remain at home in China. The strange new Forest City off the coast of Singapore that I wrote about in *Belt and Road* saw sales drop by 90%, and the few residents who had already moved in—still short of the planned 700,000 expected by 2035—quickly disappeared. Reclamation works for a second artificial island had to be postponed due to the shutdown measures imposed by Malaysia once the virus arrived in the country.[53] The pandemic seemed at first to provide an opportunity for the new freight rail lines linking China and Europe, but as some maritime and air freight orders were switched to rail, the terminals at Alashan and Khorgos, cities on the border with Kazakhstan, buckled under severe backlogs and congestion.[54]

Then there are the consequences of the global economic crisis. Loan repayments have quickly become impossible for many developing countries, particularly in Africa. In fact, China announced already in June 2020 the suspension of debt repayment for seventy-seven developing countries and regions. Beijing will have to adapt to the new facts. Finally, there is the more fundamental point that an initiative aimed at increasing China's global economic power will be considerably more difficult to execute at a time when the public in most countries has turned against globalization, blaming it for the crisis and even the pandemic. "More China" might become a difficult proposition to defend now that many blame China for the individual and collective distress brought about by the Wuhan outbreak.

On the other hand, the pandemic creates opportunities, and these seem much more significant. If one subscribes to my thesis that the Belt and Road is a revolutionary project, then the conclusion is obvious: it is much easier to bring about a revolution during periods of turmoil than during the calm. Even those loan repayment difficulties, so inconvenient at first glance, may well allow China to extract all sorts of political concessions from their troubled economic partners. In January 2021, China cancelled some of the Democratic Republic of the Congo's loans and promised to fund new projects. In return, the Central African nation joined the list of signatories to the Belt and Road. Around that time, the Chinese embassy in Nairobi announced it was conducting "smooth" talks with Kenya on alleviating its debt challenges, after the country's revenues were pummeled by the coronavirus crisis. In March 2021, with Sri Lanka facing large debt maturities by the end of the year, the Central Bank of Sri Lanka signed a currency swap agreement worth 10 billion yuan with the People's Bank of China, a way to reduce the country's reliance on the International Monetary Fund while contributing to the internationalization of the yuan.

There are three main levers that China can use to turn the pandemic into an opportunity to upturn the existing global order. The first is the direct comparison between the situation in China and elsewhere. The numbers of cases and fatalities provided by the Chinese authorities probably misrepresent the real figures by more than an order of magnitude, but the fact remains that a semblance of normalcy was achieved in a short period of time, and Chinese diplomats stationed all over the world have taken to the media to challenge America and to compare the chaos in American cities and hospitals with what they see as China's singular success in stopping the epidemic. To the extent that the United States failed to do the same meant its prestige suffered a severe blow, but one from which it will no doubt recover with a successful vaccination campaign. Which country is able to manage the recovery without increasing its own financial risks and vulnerabilities remains very much an open question.

The second lever, arguably more important, resides with industrial value chains. We saw above that Covid-19 helped consolidate China's growing dominance in important global value chains. A quick recovery from the pandemic allowed the Chinese authorities to direct recovery funds to industry and infrastructure. In Europe and the United States, political pressure and a prolonged recovery were translated into stimulus plans supporting families, employment and the consumer. In many parts of the world, political resistance to growing Chinese economic influence quickly eroded in the face of the economic crisis. As chief investment minister of Indonesia Luhut Pandjaitan put it, "we invited everybody and no one came, except the Chinese."[55] In both developing and advanced economies, the pandemic could well fuel a new worldwide wave of Chinese acquisitions at knockdown prices.

Finally, in a more extreme scenario, important countries could experience the kind of economic shock that leads to widespread social and political collapse. At that point, China would have a unique opportunity to step in, provide aid and refashion these countries in its own image. A recent agreement with Iran—including new investment projects but also Chinese access to energy and transport infrastructure—was an early sign of new opportunities. It locks in an assured source of oil and gas as China looks for a replacement for its coal plants. In February 2021, the chairman of the National People's Congress, Li Zhanshu, proposed the creation of a joint parliamentary oversight committee for the China–Pakistan Economic Corridor, the first time the initiative veered into the previously unthinkable area of political integration.[56]

We started this chapter by noting that great wars are often opportunities for the victors to reconstruct large areas of the planet according to their own models. The economic shocks resulting from the pandemic may offer an equivalent on a smaller scale, while issuing new warnings of greater shocks to come.

A TIME OF HEROES

Three or four years ago, as I drove around Beijing visiting officials and intellectuals, one message kept being repeated. In my experience, the only moment when a

Chinese intellectual or official should be taken literally is when he or she is walking his guest to his car. With no one around and no time to add any commentary, a single sentence can speak volumes. And the sentence I was hearing was this: "Always remember that China is a civilization rather than a nation state."

It was not a new idea, far from it. Nor is it an exclusively Chinese idea. But having received official sanction, the concept was being used to convey an important and often ignored message: the myth of convergence was over. From now on, China would be treading its own *Sonderweg*, its special path. As a civilization state, China is organized around the highest political concepts, irreducible to any other model.

The importance of the concept became all the more obvious to me a few months later in India, during a conversation with Ram Madhav, General Secretary of the ruling Bharatiya Janata Party. After a conference in Delhi, he explained: "From now on Asia will rule the world and that changes everything because in Asia we have civilizations rather than nations."

The exact nature of those changes was left unsaid. One immediate implication was the role of the diaspora, but the pronouncement had another meaning, much closer to home and much more consequential. By affirming that India was a separate civilization, the Modi doctrine consigned the opposition—the Indian National Congress—to the perilous role of a westernizing force, intent on measuring Indian success by the yardstick of a foreign system. The ideas that Congress had always presented as too obvious to need much defense—secularism and socialism—should be seen as cultural imports, from which India would have to free itself. What Ram Madhav was arguing was this: Asia will rule the world and that means that it will live according to its own ideas rather than Western fashions. Why should the Indian philosophical and political tradition be reinterpreted within the framework of liberalism rather than the other way around, when that tradition is thousands of years old and liberalism was born just a couple of centuries ago?

Modi was able to convince voters that they should rise against a power structure that is essentially made up of anglicized elites, and that a Western philosophy of toleration has become a symbol and a practice of contempt for Hinduism.[57] There was a time when that liberal philosophy was taken seriously almost everywhere. Many of the independence movements in what used to be called the Third World fully subscribed to it, and used the language of human rights and the rule of law against the European colonizers. The shift now taking place is arguably deeper and more radical. By accusing Western political ideas of being a sham, of masking their origin under the veneer of supposedly neutral principles, the defenders of the civilization state are saying that the search for universality is over, and that all of us must accept that we speak only for ourselves and our societies.

From the perspective of what had come before, Western political societies had oddly misplaced scientific ambitions. They wanted their political values to be accepted universally, much like a scientific theory enjoys universal validity. In order to achieve this, a monumental effort of abstraction and simplification was needed. Western civilization was to be a civilization like no other. Properly speaking, it was not to be a civilization at all, but something closer to an operating system. It should not embody a rich tapestry of traditions and customs, or pursue a religious doctrine or vision. Its principles were meant to be simple and empty, no more than an abstract framework within which different cultural possibilities could be explored. At their limit, Western values were supposed to leave everything undecided, or in other words, they were not to stand for one particular way of life against another.

The problem with Western universalism was twofold. First, Western values seemed to many people living in Asia or Africa to be just one alternative among many. The promise that traditional ways of life could be preserved in a liberal society was a fatal conceit. Were Turkey or China or Russia to import the whole set of Western values and rules, their societies would soon become replicas of the West and lose their cultural independence. While this process was seen as the necessary price for becoming modern, cultural assimilation kept its prestige, but lately many doubts have been growing about whether it is really necessary to imitate Western nations in order to acquire all the benefits of modern society. There was a second difficulty: Western values and norms still needed to be interpreted and enforced, and the most powerful nations in the West had always arrogated that task for themselves. Cultural assimilation meant political dependence.

If to all appearances we have returned to a world of civilization states, the root cause is the collapse of the concept of a world civilization. Samuel Huntington started from this realization, arguing in some of the starkest passages of his magnum opus that "the concept of a universal civilization helps justify Western cultural dominance of other societies and the need for those societies to ape Western practices and institutions."[58] Universalism is the ideology of the West for confronting other cultures. Naturally, everyone outside the West, Huntington argues, should see the idea of one world as a threat.

I believe Huntington was right, but only half right. It is true that people in Russia, China, India and many other countries increasingly see the concept of Western civilization through a different prism, as one civilization among many, with no particular claim to universality. That in itself is a mere intellectual determination. What follows is more consequential: if the West feels entitled to pursue its particular vision with all the tools of state power, why should others refrain from doing the same? Why should they refrain from building a state around their own conception of the good life, a state with a whole civilization behind it?

What Huntington failed to see was that different civilizations do not exist in order to fight, "ignorant armies clashing by night." They share a world. This might not be a normative world made up of rules and institutions, but it is a common world of natural forces to be brought under human control. The very work of civilization is to create a human world out of the natural void. The way each of them understands and pursues this task is what gives meaning to every human civilization. Huntington failed to understand this. It is as if he started from the finished work and could never retrace his steps to the origin.

Civilizations might now be too distant to share a common set of values, but they do share a common environment, too vast and too dangerous to be ignored. Have we not witnessed how the pandemic gave a specific shape to geopolitical competition? Different powers may well compete for world domination, but that also means they all belong to an increasingly integrated landscape, a general structure I call the "world game." As we shall see in the next chapter, the great questions are no longer religious or ethnic but organizational and technological, and these are the questions around which different civilizations coalesce.

We live in interesting times. Joseph Campbell would call it a time of heroes, not because there are today a greater number of exceptional individuals, but because we live in one of those moments when it becomes necessary to cross from the world of the everyday into a region of unexpected events, where familiar laws and order no longer apply. This is the elemental nature of the myths of Jason chasing the fleece over the distant seas, Aeneas in the Underworld or the young Luke Skywalker and the Star Wars galaxy. Beyond the indicated bounds lie darkness, the unknown and danger. "The familiar life horizon has been outgrown; the old concepts, ideals, and emotional patterns no longer fit; the time for the passing of a threshold is at hand."[59]

3

ESCAPE VELOCITY

One morning, as Gregor Samsa was waking up from anxious dreams, he discovered that while in bed he had been changed into a monstrous verminous bug. An unexpected and significant change, but no one, including Samsa himself, ever stopped to doubt whether he should present himself at the office in his new condition, and the firm manager even showed up at his house to inquire why he had not taken the early train.

There is something in the present moment that cannot but remind us of the opening pages of Kafka's *The Metamorphosis*. On the one hand, the pandemic has become the most significant, the most *colossal* event of our lifetimes. The activities of billions of people have been turned upside down. Events which in their time seemed world historical—think of the terrorist attacks in 2001—did not have the same impact. Every day the front pages of newspapers read like something out of an especially preposterous disaster movie. On November

22, 2020, the opening line of the evening news in the United Kingdom was: "Families will be allowed to spend Christmas together." Imagine the same headline a year before. The obvious had become breaking news, but in the end the announcement turned out to be too optimistic. On December 20, the *Sunday Times* headline read: "Christmas is cancelled by surging mutant virus."

A momentous event, we all seem to agree, but perhaps too novel for its consequences to be fully intelligible. Some even speculate that not much will change after the pandemic recedes. Covid-19 could turn out to be one of those events that occurring so completely outside the continuity of history, ends up leaving relatively few marks. Or perhaps it will indeed change the world but in a subterranean, mysterious way which we must fail to surmise: in *The Metamorphosis*, a new world arises just as people cling to the old one. Others have suggested that the pandemic could accelerate existing trends without bringing about any fundamental transformations. The problem with the latter view is that it seems to presuppose we knew where history was going before disaster hit.

Like Samsa, we feel something horrible has happened, but we still know nothing of what happens next, and are therefore tempted to continue on the same path. In the United States and Europe, in the midst of a previously unimaginable catastrophe, politics continued to be dictated by old themes and contradictions. In the United

States, Trump and the election, filtered through the lens
of the ongoing culture wars. When a band of marauders
stormed the Capitol in January 2021, the daily death toll
from the virus reached its highest figures yet; few
noticed. In Europe, all the important issues from the
previous year were carried into 2020: Brexit, immigra-
tion and Turkey, the rule of law in Central and Eastern
Europe, and even the old and arcane debate about strategic autonomy.

As hard to understand as that may be, there is no
monument in the main world capitals to the victims of
the Spanish flu, a pandemic responsible for as many as
100 million deaths a century ago. It is difficult to assign
great historical meaning to a pandemic, which is perhaps why they tend to be forgotten. What most people
seem to crave is to return to normality. "Unlike the end
of the second world war in Europe, our cities do not
need physically rebuilding. We can look around us, and
imagine the pandemic never happened."[1] For many others, however, the current pandemic is a state of emergency, and it opens "the possibility, so long sought after
in futile and periodic gestures, for sudden profound
transformation."[2]

The editorial board of the *Financial Times*—sometimes presented as a symbol of convention and conserva-
tism—was among the first to call for revolution or, at
least, radical reforms: "Radical reforms will need to be
put on the table." The salmon-tinted broadsheet saw in

the pandemic an opportunity to reverse the prevailing policy direction of the last four decades.[3]

The old individualism suddenly looked crass. Faced with an existential threat, societies pulled together and grave inequalities were exposed afresh. Workers in essential services and healthcare now look critical to our survival, but their economic realities do not reflect that fact. The economic lockdowns are imposing the greatest cost on those already worst off, making existing inequalities clearly unsustainable. The 57.3% of the American population employed in November 2020 was still at the lowest level since May 1983, after months of recovery and up from 51.3% in April. Meanwhile, America's wealthiest saw their fortunes soar. The hundred richest people in the U.S. added about US$600 billion to their wealth in 2020.[4] Between March and the end of the year, the United States gained 56 new billionaires, according to the Institute for Policy Studies, bringing the total to 659.

The pandemic exposed deep inequalities. It also aggravated them. In Beverly Hills and Palo Alto, public school teachers were enticed away to teach single children from affluent families as a way to eliminate the risks of going to school.[5] In March 2020, when medical equipment in the United States was in dramatically short supply, a small ventilator company near Seattle "received enquiries from a number of wealthy individuals hoping to buy their own personal ventilators, a fallback plan in case the American hospital system buckles."[6]

The weakness of the response was directly connected to the brittleness of our social and economic arrangements. If governments had taken on a greater responsibility for the common good and if tax policy had given them the resources to pursue it, would we have found ourselves so unprepared to deal with the emergency? Would doctors and nurses in hospitals across Europe and the United States have been forced to risk their lives in the absence of adequate protective equipment? And if a universal basic income had already been in place, would the need to impose social restrictions in order to contain the epidemic have carried the same economic and social cost?

Those who sensed a historical state of emergency were quick to describe the pandemic as a capitalist product—or excrescence. "Capital is fastened to ever more land and sucking its contents into circulation at an ever madder pace, and this must, as a general law, result in a high risk of zoonotic pandemics—diseases passing from animal to human—as one consequence of the ecological havoc caused."[7] The message is that one cannot expect to leave the pandemic behind—or a world riddled with pandemics and other disasters—without at the same time leaving the capitalist system behind.

THE END OF CAPITALISM?

Radical reforms will be put on the table, starting with a much greater role for governments. To those who argue that the Covid-19 crisis exposes the failure not of the market, but of state structures, one possible response is that the state failed because of an economic system that permanently saps its powers and capacity. We seem to have realized some of the darkest prophecies of cyberpunk: large multinationals are increasingly in charge and even governments are forced to behave like companies, small chinks in vast but fragile supply chains. Israel offered Pfizer access to biodata from its citizens in exchange for vaccine doses.[8] Denmark tried a similar bargain. During the worst weeks of the pandemic, the wealthy retreated to private worlds insulated from every contagion source. The spaces that still created common experiences were increasingly abandoned or even shut down, and the services booming in 2020 and 2021 were the ones keeping different classes apart. Will the coronavirus crisis be followed by the same forces of resistance and revolution foretold by novelists such as Bruce Sterling and William Gibson?

As the pandemic economic crisis first hit, the European Union put in place or activated short-term work schemes, while Americans received generous stimulus checks that on average actually increased disposable income. In time, temporary measures gave way to bolder ideas. Already in May 2020, responding to what was quickly dubbed the most dramatic economic crisis in the history of the Union, the European Commission proposed a new €750 billion recovery instrument, embedded within the multiannual budget. The money was raised by borrowing €750 billion on capital markets. A new Recovery and Resilience Facility with a budget of €672.5 billion distributed in grants and loans will form the main pillar of the recovery plan. This will support member states as they implement investments and reforms that are essential for a sustainable recovery. A common political responsibility is assumed, although strictly speaking no national debt liability is taken on beyond what they are already committed to deliver in the current budget cycle. More importantly, perhaps, member states are not expected to repay those debts according to the same key used to apportion the initial grants. In other words, the plan envisages a form of fiscal transfer from wealthier countries to those most directly affected by the crisis.

When Joe Biden announced his new infrastructure plan and corporate tax rise in April, he vouched the goal was to create the strongest and most innovative economy in the world. He added that geopolitics, not class politics, was the main driver: "It will promote our national security interest and put us in a position to win the global competition with China in the upcoming years." US$180 billion of funds will be directed towards investments in research and development in areas such as artificial intelligence and biotechnology, aimed at improving competitiveness with China. A further US$300 billion in government spending is to be devoted to manufacturing subsidies targeted at semiconductors and other strategic industries.[9] A few months into his presidency, Joe Biden is lauded as the man responsible for the "dawn of a new economic era," someone fated to "reengineer America." Progressives have been waiting decades now for the coming of a new myth, a figure that can, as Eric Levitz puts it, exorcise the ghost of Reagan from American politics and "raise the New Deal Order from its grave." The pandemic "reinforced this intellectual fashion for a new economic order, while appearing to open up political space for its construction."[10]

The transformation was no less visible in Asia, and it took place somewhat faster. For decades, as James Crabtree argues, leaders of the most successful economies in Asia spoke proudly of their small, nimble administrations. While European welfare states were bloated and inefficient, Asian governments were thrifty, scientific and, more importantly, small enough not to sap the energies and drive of their citizens. Singapore, not known for its budget extravagance, spent more than US$100 billion in 2020 on everything from cash handouts to public support for struggling airlines, hotels and the construction sector. Myanmar unveiled measures adding up to about 2% of GDP, a remarkable sum for a country where tax revenues add up to a paltry 5% of GDP. In July 2020, Bank Indonesia shocked investors with plans to buy up US$40 billion of its own government bonds, in effect monetizing public debt.[11]

At the height of the lockdowns, roughly one fourth to one third of our economies were put on pause. Moving forward, there is no doubt that many things will have to change. Some percentage of the recent layoffs will result in permanent job loss. Indeed, even as the job market in developed economies is creating opportunities at a faster clip than most economists expected, a surge in registrations for training suggests workers anticipate fundamental shifts in the labor market. Whole sectors have been singled out for closure. Others will be created anew. The path back to full employment will be arduous.

For many on the radical left and the radical right, this is the doctrine they have been preaching. If whole economies can be reprogramed to eliminate the risk of a viral infection, then it must be possible to do the same for the sake of other, equally desirable social purposes. When the virus arrived, the same authorities who had always claimed nothing could be done about homelessness quickly found the resources to house the indigent. Water and electricity bills could wait after all, paid sick leave was possible and late mortgage payments did not lead to foreclosure. "America's response to the coronavirus pandemic has revealed a simple truth: So many policies that our elected officials have long told us were impossible and impractical were eminently possible and practical all along."[12]

Faced with an unprecedented challenge, businesses reacted remarkably well, most notably the biotechnology and pharmaceutical companies developing new vaccine technologies in record time. The list includes other important achievements: keeping grocery store shelves stocked even as much of the capacity to process and distribute food was disrupted; redeploying factories to make ventilators and medical equipment and keeping transport or logistics systems up and running in the face of mammoth challenges. As one writer puts it:

> In many cities, when a sudden rainstorm arrives, street vendors of cheap umbrellas will appear as if out of nowhere, driven not by some central authority but responding to the invisible hand of the marketplace. If you substitute masks for umbrellas, and substitute apparel companies for street hawkers, you have a fair description of the magic of the marketplace in 2020.[13]

The magic of the marketplace? None of this had anything to do with the spontaneous interplay of individual economic units that economists like to talk about. In fact, it comes remarkably close to what Hayek called an organization, something akin to a collective mind. In some cases, the government took over the function of reorganizing economic activity; in others, large dominant platforms performed that task. The internet brought the leading actors together and helped them align their views and methods. Any resistance from opposing interests was effectively coopted or overcome.

At the beginning of the pandemic in Europe and North America, the widespread fear that economic and social life would be irreparably damaged prompted many consumers to stock up on essential goods. Photos and videos circulated on social media showing long lines outside supermarkets and empty shelves inside. As amateur economists, we all knew one thing: given a deep enough external shock, the economy could well collapse like a house of cards.

Instead, supply chains adapted and readjusted at extraordinary speed. At the end of 2019, only around 13% of retail purchases in the United States were made online, according to Mastercard. By the end of 2020, that figure stood at around 20%. Before the pandemic, when e-ecommerce growth rates averaged between 12% and 16% annually, that kind of jump would have taken several years to happen. Covid was the final nail in the coffin for several department store chains and created the need for new shopping models. Supermarket giant Walmart rolled out new test stores that function as both physical shopping destinations and online fulfilment centers.

Demand for robotics exploded, especially in the food supply chain. If workers are kept at home or unable to travel across borders because of the pandemic, machines that can harvest and deliver food are an obvious solution. In other cases, there has been a surge in demand for disinfection robots, equipped with tools such as ultraviolet light to kill viruses. There are many similar examples where the latest technology is helping limit disruption to supply chains.

A few years ago, Marc Andreessen argued that software was eating the world. He described a dramatic and broad technological and economic shift in which software companies took over large swaths of the economy. Software was even swallowing much of the value chain of industries such as automobiles, that are widely viewed as primarily existing in the physical world.

That process may now be so advanced that the best way to think about the economy is as the longest computer program in the world, composed of continuously evolving, and manipulable, lines of code. That should not be understood as a license to just follow our wishes. These lines of code are interconnected, and even the smallest bug, if left undetected, can lead to a system crash. What the metaphor promises is the ability to control and change our circumstances. Ultimately, we stand outside the economic system, and it can be changed in strikingly new ways.

That a deadly pathogen could quickly spread all over the world was not surprising. The scenario had been part of policy planning exercises for two or three decades. We knew something resembling the current pandemic was bound to happen in a world where zoonotic sources of infection are prevalent and where the speed and depth of global connections have increased markedly since the turn of the century. No one can exclude the possibility that a deadlier pandemic will take place in the future.

What I believe took even the most seasoned observer by surprise was the political response. That a modern megapolis such as Wuhan could be placed under a strict lockdown came as a shock, but back then it was still possible to interpret the response as a peculiarity of the Chinese communist regime and to believe that nothing of the kind could be expected to happen in free societies. When similar measures were applied in Italy and then all across Europe and North America, a number of powerful assumptions were decisively refuted. We are still grappling with the consequences.

The new coronavirus achieved in days what both progressives and nationalists had long been fighting for. Powerful economic interests were sidelined, whole industries had to temporarily close down, oil consumption plummeted, national borders were closed and export bans imposed. It was a humbling experience, as the ripples of politics paled in comparison to the giant natural wave of the pandemic, but also a conversion moment, where one could finally see the social and economic system for what it is. The great pause revealed a hidden truth, and once revealed, it cannot be forgotten.

What has come to an end is not capitalism but the idea of capitalism as a system standing above economic agents. With the Spanish flu a century ago, people adapted their individual behavior, but social life proceeded more or less as before. "Public places of amusement" were shuttered, but work and business were little affected overall. Many workers suffered, dying in factories and mines; but in the United States, real gross national product actually grew in 1919, albeit by a modest 1%. Retail was barely affected, and businesses did not declare bankruptcy at unusual rates.

With the coronavirus, the response was very different. Abruptly and with little notice, the economy was put on pause. In part, that is because we now have the tools to do so: the internet and other information and logistics technologies to keep essential services going, and activist central banks and governments to manage the resulting economic shock. The illusion that the economy is an organic entity outside of social control was tacitly shattered. It is not surprising, in this context, that the Biden administration would look for ways to reform a broken international corporate tax system. The plan features a 15% global minimum corporate tax rate and a proposal to reallocate some tax paid by the largest, most profitable companies to countries where they make their sales. In April, *The Economist* announced that "as the economy emerges from the pandemic, a reversal of the primacy of capital over labor beckons."[14]

A health official in the United Kingdom explained that at first, no restrictive measures were put in place because no one knew it was possible—let alone easy, as he put it—to impose a lockdown in a modern society. Without the pandemic, we might never have found out. Like the hero of a Bildungsroman, we had to wait for an unexpected crisis to discover the true extent of our powers. The crisis will leave scars, but also awaken new and unsuspected forces.

THE END OF GLOBALIZATION?

If the market has lost its place at the apex of the social order, it seems doubtful that the state will be able to replace it. The current moment is starting to look like a spy thriller. The crisis of capitalism would seem to point to the emergence or reemergence of the state as the main principle of order, but when we turn in that direction, we soon discover that the state has not been able to assert itself against the forces of globalization, and we start to suspect the existence of a hidden actor.

A popular view is that the virus revealed the problems with the current globalization model. Global value chains are as efficient as they are fragile, while air travel made us all vulnerable to rapidly growing epidemics. Capital flows have increased competition between tax jurisdictions, depriving states of tax revenue. For many on both the left and the right, a return to a world where states are allowed to exert greater levels of control over their own borders and economies is a necessary first step if we want to avoid future pandemics. Perhaps, according to those critics, the current crisis will be regarded as the beginning of the end of globalization.

Let us look at the evidence.

When the pandemic started, analysts warned that container lines could lose more than US$20 billion in 2020. As it turned out, profits exceeded US$14 billion, a value not seen in almost a decade. Relative to its level in August 2019, world trade hit bottom in May 2020, when it had reached a cumulative decline of 17.6%. In the next few months, however, trade flows grew at a fast pace. Already, by August, the year-on-year decline had been reduced to 4.4%. In March 2021, the World Trade Organization revised up its estimate of the volume of world goods trade to a fall of just 5.3% for the whole of 2020, and predicted an 8% growth in 2021. Trade economists tell us that the reason for the quick recovery is that the trade collapse earlier in the year did not operate at the extensive margin. Firms reduced the volume of international trade, but the global networks—measured by number of international firms rather than volume of activity—were essentially preserved. Even accounting for persistently high levels of uncertainty about the timing and effectiveness of a vaccine, it seems reasonable that the shock was widely perceived to be more transitory than the Great Recession. As a result, it was natural that firms were unwilling to sever international ties and to reshore activity domestically.[15]

This does not mean businesses everywhere have not adjusted their strategies. The challenge will be to balance efficiency and security, or to make supply chains more resilient without weakening their competitiveness. There is a lesson to be taken from the energy industry. Because energy is so tightly connected to national security, and because every sector relies on energy inputs, the concern with energy security has always been present. What is happening after the pandemic is that other sectors—

pharmaceuticals and critical medical supplies, for example, but also semiconductors—may now follow a similar logic by either diversifying supplies or stockpiling key inputs or items. A report from McKinsey shows that companies now expect a month-long disruption to hit their supply chains once every 3.7 years, be that from climate change, cyber-attacks, political unrest or trade wars.[16] In March 2021, a single stranded ship was able to block the southern entrance to the Suez Canal, forcing container liners and oil tankers to contemplate sending their cargo around the southern tip of Africa, adding at least a week to shipping times. The *Ever Given* held up an estimated US$10 billion of goods a day. As one wit put it, the global supply chain is thousands of miles long but only an eighth of an inch deep.[17] As of March 26, some 237 vessels, including oil tankers and dozens of container ships, were waiting to transit the canal, which handles about 12% of global trade.

The *Ever Given* affair followed a series of developments impairing the smooth functioning of global supply chains. By the end of 2020, carmakers in Europe and the United States suddenly realized they were facing a shortage of chips used in vehicles, because semiconductor manufacturers had allocated more capacity to meet soaring demand from consumer electronics. Lockdowns and travel restrictions prompted housebound consumers to snap up more phones, game consoles and laptops to get online. Volkswagen said that the bottlenecks meant it would produce 100,000 fewer cars in the first quarter of 2021 at sites in Europe, North America and China, because its parts makers Continental and Bosch have struggled to secure supplies from their contractors.[18] Toyota announced in January it was partially halting production in China, while Honda reduced output at five factories across North America.[19] By May 2021, the deepening global chip crunch had spread to makers of smartphones, televisions and home appliances. At the same time, the huge second wave in India posed a new threat to the global shipping industry, which relies on the country for seafarers, after crews came down with the disease and major ports such as Singapore banned the entry of ships.[20] It was a vivid example of the vulnerabilities of global value chains after Covid, and the shock waves are likely to continue. A world that worries more about security than low prices is one that will likely deliver lower productivity and higher prices, but that is fully compatible with superior social outcomes.

The change could be difficult. All the examples in recent decades show that building a new supplier infrastructure is a long and complex process. On the one hand, the pandemic has exposed unsustainable levels of dependency on the Chinese manufacturing base. On the other, that dependency is not a product of chance or neutral historical forces. Heavily supported by government incentives, it took twenty years for China to build a local base capable of supplying the vast majority of electronic components, auto parts, chemicals and drug ingredients needed for domestic manufacturing. Shifting production away from China will be just as difficult. The second strategy—safety stockpiling—will carry costs and risks but seems inevitable, particularly in those sectors where one can expect significant political pressure to avoid the catastrophic failures seen during the Covid pandemic.[21] An adequate response to a crisis of this magnitude cannot be left to the private sector alone.

Notice that neither strategy relies on notions of economic nationalism or obvious forms of reshoring. The reason should be obvious: economic nationalism would be counterproductive. Take the case of Samsung Electronics. Its main plant is near the city of Daegu, the epicenter of an early virus outbreak at the end of February 2020. The outbreak forced frequent shutdowns of its home plant, causing disruption to premium smartphone production for the local market. The response, interestingly, was to move out, with the company shifting part of its domestic phone production to Vietnam where it operates other factories.[22] Global companies with highly complex supply chains boast better and faster information systems—control towers and mapping tools—providing accurate real-time information on production networks, and these tools allow for an efficient management of risks. As Peter Williamson has argued, capacity designed to supply a local market will be smaller scale and have fewer options to dramatically increase production in response to a crisis than a network of suppliers spanning different countries and regions.[23]

In an obvious sense, globalization will come out of the pandemic in even stronger shape. The virus shock has, as a general rule, been met with a retreat or escape from the physical world into virtual life, where national borders tend to dissolve. By intensifying the dash to digital, the pandemic gave a powerful boost to a critical pillar of globalization: information flows. Cross-border internet traffic jumped 48% from mid-2019 to mid-2020, twice the annual rate seen in the previous three years.[24]

There will be many more digital nomads after the pandemic. If those working from home rise to 8% or 10% of the workforce in the United States and Europe, and if only 10% of them choose to move to a different country or even live without a fixed address, that will be a large and powerful new global elite. One hotel company recently started a monthly subscription service called "global passport," which allows members to stay at any of its twenty-one properties around the world at any time for a US$1,500 monthly fee instead of nightly fees. The program requires a minimum of seven and a maximum of twenty-nine nights at any one location.[25] The new digital mobility will have consequences for local and national finances. If the mega rich become even less attached to a particular geography than they already are, the global competition for capital and talent will continue to intensify.

It is helpful to think of the changes brought about by the pandemic in this schematic way: Covid added a new layer of complexity to the existing system, while preserving all its previous elements. States are still connected by global relations of production and consumption, but those relations no longer exist in a void. Global markets are no longer the justifying principle of the system, but neither have states retreated to a national orbit. Rather, a new overarching principle has emerged: the environment or nature. Suddenly, both globalization and capitalism appear as tools deployed for mastering or controlling the natural environment. Since this environment has no national borders, a global approach is prima facie justified, but globalization is not an end in itself. Similarly, capitalism must be interpreted in its original meaning as a rational method designed to increase our control over natural forces; for John Locke, the system of property is based on economic growth through the conquest of nature. The crisis of the system is simply its forced rediscovery of a "lost world."

The main question posed by the Covid-19 pandemic will be the one concerning technology. The responses adopted by governments around the world seem to fall into two main categories. Those countries able to leverage new and emerging technologies to fight the virus have done better at limiting the number of cases and fatalities, while managing to keep most of their economies and societies operational. The countries unable to use technology had to rely on lockdowns, quarantines, generalized closures and other physical restrictions—the same methods used to fight the Spanish flu more than a century ago, and in many cases, with the same slow, painful results. In Singapore and South Korea, individuals were digitally monitored, but life often felt normal, or almost normal. In Spain and Italy, as in many other parts of Europe and the United States, people were not monitored, but for long periods they were not supposed to leave home.

The question becomes more interesting and more complicated after one realizes that those countries that more clearly struggled with the social uses of technology were able to rely on their scientific bases and pools of capital to develop new vaccines and even new vaccine technologies. Vaccine developers were able to cut the typical production time for a vaccine from more than ten years to under one, while spending billions on the effort. BioNTech, the small biotech company based in Germany, simply plugged the genetic code for the spike protein protruding from the surface of the coronavirus into its software. We used to grow vaccines. Now we print them. Many were skeptical of the new messenger ribonucleic technology (mRNA), which had never been used in an approved product. The pandemic made both researchers and company executives a lot bolder.

The virus outbreak has brought to the surface a fact that many of us have long suspected: the backlash against technology in the West has become the main threat to its security and prosperity—just as other regions are embracing technological progress—but in the process, the pandemic also worked as a wake-up call and a spur to faster technological development.

If we come out of this crisis with a single widely shared belief, if some previously ignored idea could become a new consensus, it will likely be a recognition that the history of technology is far from concluded. There is no way to stop technological progress, even if, by hypothesis, we were happy with the current plateau. The coronavirus proved that our natural environment continues to be as dangerous and hostile to human life as it has always been.

Of course, the ongoing public debate about climate change pointed to the same conclusion, but with a critical difference: climate change seemed to show that human activity was the problem, or that technology was the problem. The coronavirus turns this intuition on its head. Far from believing that our natural environment needs to be liberated from human interference, we are now much more likely to think that it needs to be colonized anew. Nature is once again the problem. The present moment feels like a beginning, almost as if humanity is once again entering the Neolithic.

THE GREAT ACCELERATION

The beginning of the second year of the pandemic brought yet another troubling novelty: the appearance of potentially more infectious virus variants carrying the threat that, with just one wrong mutation, the new vaccines could be rendered powerless. First, a SARS-CoV-2 variant emerged in the UK that had acquired seventeen mutations, including eight in the spike. An apparently independent lineage emerged in South Africa that also had multiple spike mutations. An analysis by Public Health England showed about 15% of the contacts of people infected with the B.1.1.7 variant in England went on to test positive themselves, compared with 10% of contacts of those infected with other variants. In January, the American Centers for Disease Control and Prevention (CDC) issued a report with a modeled trajectory of B.1.1.7 where it became the predominant variant in March, and the same process quickly happened in Europe. Even with no known difference in clinical outcomes associated with known variants, a higher rate of transmission leads to more cases, increasing the number of persons who need clinical care, exacerbating the burden on an already strained healthcare system and resulting in more deaths. The report quietly noted the appearance of a first case of SARS-CoV-2 reinfection in Brazil with a SARS-CoV-2 variant that contained the E484K mutation, which has been shown to reduce neutralization by convalescent sera and monoclonal antibodies.

In March, a new variant known as B.1.617 quickly became dominant in the Indian state of Maharashtra. B.1.617 drew concern because it contained two mutations linked to increased transmissibility and an ability to evade immune protection. A variant of lineage B.1.617 known as Delta quickly spread worldwide. Much more contagious than previous strains, it posed a formidable challenge to the health systems of Russia, Indonesia, Bangladesh, and many other countries. By July 2021, it had been confirmed in 96 countries. In 20 countries around the world there was a new exponential increase of infections. A study produced by the Israel's health ministry, details of which were made public in July, suggested the Pfizer vaccine provides only 64 per cent protection against symptomatic infection with Delta.

It is essentially a numbers game: the more virus that is circulating, the more chance mutants have to appear. In a survey of seventy-seven epidemiologists carried out by the People's Vaccine Alliance in March 2021, two thirds thought we had a year or less before the virus mutates to the extent that the majority of first-generation vaccines are rendered ineffective and new vaccines are required.

The threat of immune escape was significant. It set up a race between vaccination and virus mutation, suggesting that the pandemic might yet take new and ominous turns. The logic of emergency was reinforced. Perhaps a full return to normal would prove impossible: the urgent need now is to expect the worst and prepare for the worst. Biomedical research and innovation should be accelerated to reduce the likelihood of future and even greater threats arising from a quickly evolving situation, while genomic surveillance has become an imperative. Without it, we have no idea what is really happening.

The virus could perhaps be seen as a fluke, implausible as the thesis might be. But as the pandemic progressed, there seemed to be a greater awareness that, in one way or another, the state of emergency would last. The new war against nature will last longer than was hoped. And if that is true, our approach to technology needs to change.

That approach has changed often in the past, so a new transformation would not be surprising. I agree with those authors who have spoken in recent years of a "Great Stagnation", a technological plateau requiring much greater exertions than in the past to achieve fast economic growth. We started to exhaust the benefits of our previous momentum, while taking those benefits for granted. As Tyler Cowen put it in his classic *The Great Stagnation*, "The new model is that there are periodic technological plateaus, and right now we are sitting on top of one, waiting for the next major growth revolution." He was writing in 2011, and already the intuition then was that only a major societal shock could shake us out of our complacency. Technology had become a bit of a luxury, noticed more often for the problems it caused than for the benefits it had brought about. Those benefits were, after all, not so recent that one could remember the world before them. As Cowen wrote:

> The period from 1880 to 1940 brought numerous major technological advances into our lives. The long list of new developments includes electricity, electric

lights, powerful motors, automobiles, airplanes, house-hold appliances, the telephone, indoor plumbing, phar-maceuticals, mass production, the typewriter, the tape recorder, the phonograph, and radio, to name just a few, with television coming at the end of that period. The railroad and fast international ships were not com-pletely new, but they expanded rapidly during this period, tying together the world economy.[26]

These new technologies had quite a lot in common, exploring a generalized technology to the end: advanced machines combined with fossil fuels.

More recent decades have been disappointing. Compared to what people experienced in the past, our technologies are better versions of old things and the pace of change has slowed down markedly. Yes, we have the internet, but so far it has proven more of a boon for the intellectually curious than for the industrious or the revolutionary. So far, the internet has only interpreted the world, but the goal is to change it.

As Robert Gordon argued almost a decade ago, "invention since 2000 has centered on entertainment and communication devices that are smaller, smarter, and more capable, but do not fundamentally change labor productivity or the standard of living in the way that electric light, motor cars, or indoor plumbing changed it." Gordon famously asked us to consider the following thought experiment: would you prefer to keep everything invented in the past decade but have to give up running water and indoor toilets, or keep the latter and give up the incredible fruits of the internet? He thought the answer was obvious a decade ago—his audiences always laughed when he posed the question—and it might still be obvious today. Just one of those hit inventions of the Second Industrial Revolution beats all the electronic portable devices on which we have become so dependent.[27]

Perhaps the pandemic could begin to change that. The first set of links is rather direct. With the economic downturn, the pressure for short-term financial results has temporarily abated and many companies are using the moment to invest in new technology. The pandemic may not have brought about new ideas of doing business, but it gave a decisive boost to ideas that were already available, with many services seeing unprecedented bursts in digitization. In 2020, grocery delivery grew by more than 10% in China, the United Kingdom and the United States. The more digital companies and services become, the more automated they need to be, so Covid-19 has also expanded the role and promise of robotics. Some surveys suggest that in the United States at least, the share of firms with fully automated fulfilment centers may rise by 50% within a year.

Many psychological obstacles to technological development are crumbling at the same time. I group them into two areas, both related to our state of emergency, the "end time" psychology of the present moment. First, we have realized that time is actually scarce. Moving fast is the responsible choice, now that we understand deadly threats can arrive suddenly and catch us unprepared. Second, societies have a collective responsibility to address common problems, and consent cannot become a veto power held by each individual that affects our ability to act collectively. Peter Thiel, a card-carrying member of the Great Stagnation society, sees an epochal change, telling *Forbes* magazine: "I keep thinking the other side of it is that one should think of Covid and the crisis of this year as this giant watershed moment, where this is the first year of the 21st century. This is the year in which the new economy is actually replacing the old economy." Thiel thinks that the historical transformation promised by the internet was aborted in March 2000 when the tech bubble burst. It was too early. "But I keep thinking that maybe this time the movie is going to have the alternate ending—which is somehow the tech is actually going to work, at least in the aggregate," he says. "Some will fail, some won't, but on the whole, the transformation of the 21st century is going to work."[28]

There are some unmistakable signs that technological change is about to accelerate. Some of these are directly related to the pandemic. The ability to encode and deploy messenger RNA in our bodies will have applications far beyond the new vaccines now being used against Covid-19. The value of mRNA lies less in the specific products developed than in the platform, whose range of applications can only be guessed at at present. Both Moderna and BioNTech have vaccine candidates targeting cancer. BioNTech reported in 2017 that all of the first thirteen people with advanced-stage melanoma to receive the personalized immunotherapy showed elevated immunity against the mutated bits of their tumors. Moderna reported similar findings. For their cancer vaccines, algorithms compare the DNA sequences of the two samples and produce a list of thirty-four targets, each encoding a different mutant protein expressed by the cancer that is predicted to be useful in training the immune system to attack the disease.[29] The first vaccine to fully immunize against malaria uses a similar platform, instructing the body to create the protein in the *Plasmodium* parasite responsible for inhibiting memory T-cells. The patent was published in February 2021 under the title "Uses of Parasite Macrophage Migration Inhibitory Factors."

As the pandemic raged, DeepMind announced that its AI system AlphaFold had been recognized as a solution to an old problem in biology: protein folding. In his acceptance speech for the 1972 Nobel Prize in Chemistry, Christian Anfinsen postulated that a protein's amino acid sequence should fully determine its structure. This hypothesis sparked a five-decade quest to be able to computationally predict a protein's physical structure based solely on its amino acid sequence. DeepMind trained its system on publicly available data consisting of tens of thousands of protein structures from the Protein Data Bank, together with large databases containing protein sequences of unknown structure. By iterating this process, the system develops strong predictions of the underlying physical structure of the protein, and is able to determine highly accurate structures in a matter of days.[30] Being able to know the structure of every protein the human body can produce should allow us to determine which molecules would be good candidate drugs. It will also allow us to map the structures of new virus proteins or to understand ageing at a cellular level. The breakthrough was remarkable not just because of its predictable impact on biomedicine and health, but also because it showed, perhaps for the first time, what machine learning could truly achieve. As Eli Dourado noted, most applications of machine learning so far are essentially toys.[31] Protein folding is the real deal: superhuman machine intelligence in the service of world-transforming technology. Expect a lot more of it.

If the Great Stagnation does come to an end, should we credit Covid as a factor? The answer is most probably yes, because the pandemic is visibly changing our calculations when it comes to technological development. We tend to be more open to risk and disruption when they are present all around us, and the success of the new vaccines is making everyone more positive about technological development and its obvious achievements. I would also speculate that the pandemic will teach us to think more aptly and rigorously about counterfactuals. The economic and social gains from the Covid vaccines should be measured not against the state of the world before the pandemic, but against a future state of the world where no vaccines had been discovered. As we increasingly turn to clean sources of energy, the same logic applies: "Similarly, clean energy that hypothetically has the exact same energy density and cost as fossil fuels but does not entail the same social cost of carbon mostly shows itself in the avoided counterfactual of a worse world with even more severe climate change disasters."[32]

As we look around us, breakthroughs in energy and transportation are happening at breakneck speed, and the only question is whether our societies will be willing to pay the costs and run the risks of sponsoring a full-scale transition to new technological and economic systems. At the end of 2020, Waymo announced the launch of a taxi service that is fully driverless and open to the public. Walmart announced in December that it planned to use fully autonomous box trucks to make deliveries in Arkansas, starting in 2021.[33] As retail goes online as a result of the pandemic, massive delivery volumes are now placing pressure on existing models. Some retail companies are turning to a new kind of delivery driver to get packages to customers in time: their own employees. There is an obvious connection between Covid and the increasingly irresistible appeal of driverless vehicles.

In September 2020, the *New York Times* reported that "scientists developing a compact version of a nuclear fusion reactor have shown in a series of research papers that it should work, renewing hopes that the long-elusive goal of mimicking the way the sun produces energy might be achieved and eventually contribute to the fight against climate change."[34] Geothermal power seems poised for a big breakout. With better drilling technology, it may finally be ready to scale up and become a major player in clean energy. In fact, if its more enthusiastic backers are correct, geothermal may hold the key to making 100% clean electricity available to everyone in the world.[35] In April 2021, Prometheus announced it was ready to launch a new technology capable of capturing carbon dioxide from the atmosphere at just US$36 per ton. By 2030, the 500,000 fuel forges the company expects to have running will have captured a whopping 6.7 GT of carbon dioxide.

Boom Supersonic, a startup, will fly a supersonic aircraft in 2021. Airbus has given itself five years to develop a commercially viable hydrogen aircraft, a Herculean task that will require reinventing the whole aviation industry.[36] With Starlink revenue, SpaceX could be working on a human mission to Mars by the end of the decade. In the meantime, China has recently announced it is developing a mission to send a pair of spacecraft to study the far reaches of the solar system and to reach interstellar space by 2049, the magical year when the

People's Republic celebrates a hundred years of existence.[37] Two researchers from Cambridge and Columbia have even suggested building a space elevator they called the "Spaceline": "by extending a line, anchored on the moon, to deep within Earth's gravity well, we can construct a stable, traversable cable allowing free movement from the vicinity of Earth to the Moon's surface."[38] What I like about this project is that it is both feasible and revolutionary, forcing us to think outside existing frameworks. We find more and more of these kinds of ideas being seriously discussed.

The pandemic was also the moment when Bitcoin went mainstream. Having continued to grow and solidify in previous years, the cryptocurrency was perhaps always destined for a successful year, but Covid made an obvious contribution. As central banks announced larger and larger stimulus packages, Bitcoin was suddenly a shield against inflationary dynamics. Dollar weakness was a dominant factor, but for many investors it was also a question of looking in new directions after traditional investment strategies failed to respond to a radically unexpected external shock.

One of the most famous quant analysts on Wall Street announced in October 2020 that investment strategies relying on historical data could not survive in a world gone mad. "At their core, quant funds try to apply backtests to future investment decisions. But what does it mean to do quant research and run backtests if the rules have changed?"[39]

"Quants rely on data from time periods that have no reflection of today's environment," said Adam Taback, chief investment officer of Wells Fargo Private Wealth Management. "When you have volatility in markets, it makes it extremely difficult for them to catch anything because they get whipsawed back and forth." Renaissance Technologies, which manages the world's biggest quant hedge fund, saw a decline of about 20% through October 2020 in its long-biased fund. The firm, founded by former codebreaker Jim Simons, told investors that its losses were due to being under-hedged during March's collapse and then over-hedged in the rebound from April through June. "It is not surprising that our funds, which depend on models that are trained on historical data, should perform abnormally in a year that is anything but normal by historical standards," Renaissance told clients in a September letter seen by Bloomberg.[40]

In some parts of the investor community, Bitcoin is regarded as the last functioning fire alarm warning us of the dangers threatening the dollar's stability as the global reserve currency. As the only asset whose price is not under direct or indirect control by the Federal Reserve, its astonishing rise in the last two years could be the only available indicator of the looming prospect of debt monetization in the United States and a collapse in the value of the dollar.[41] The whole world seemed to be following a massive incentive to borrow dollars, buy Bitcoin and settle the debt after the value of the Bitcoin holdings and borrowed dollars had meaningfully diverged. And why not? One currency was becoming increasingly scarce, the other was decaying over time as a result of momentary inflation.

A once-in-a-generation calamity like the coronavirus was bound to create extreme gyrations in global markets, with some assets proving big winners and some losing big. In hindsight, Bitcoin was the biggest winner from the coronavirus crisis of 2020, with few analysts projecting that the economy will return to its former dynamics anytime soon.[42] Investors such as Paul Tudor Jones and Stanley Druckenmiller have thrown their weight behind it, and crypto-focused hedge funds have outshone their peers. Square, the payments company, said it would put some US$50 million, or 1% of its assets, into the cryptocurrency. PayPal, another payments company, announced it would allow its 346 million customers to hold Bitcoin and other cryptocurrencies, and to use the digital assets to shop at the 26 million merchants on its network. In December, crypto exchange Coinbase filed with regulators to go public. Prices for Bitcoin shot past US$20,000 on December 16, setting a new price record, and within days it had surpassed US$23,000. At the beginning of 2021, the price finally crossed US$30,000, reaching an all-time high of—yes—US$63,000 in April, ahead of the spectacular Coinbase debut.

4

A NEW PLANET

The Neolithic is a historical category used for classifying and studying ancient human societies, but today we are inclined to merge historical and geological periods, as if humanity had become nature and nature had acquired human traits. The new concept of the Anthropocene refers to the geological epoch when human action has become the dominant force shaping the planet, or in other words, when human beings become a geological force. I use the maximalist definition first proposed by Paul Crutzen. It would be possible to speak of human action as just one cause of environmental change among many others, but in that case there would be nothing special about the last two or three centuries. Thousands of years ago, humans had already emitted sufficient greenhouse gases—by deforestation, rice cultivation and cattle breeding—to change the global climate.[1] And when Europeans carried smallpox and other diseases to the Americas, the death of more than 50 million people over a few decades led to farmland returning to forest over such an extensive area that the growing trees sucked enough carbon dioxide out of the atmosphere to cool the planet.[2]

If the Anthropocene is to survive as a distinctive concept, we need to accept the simple definition according to which human action has replaced natural forces to such an extent that we now live primarily within human rather than natural systems, the latter being subordinate to or embedded within the former. This simple definition, however, is impossible to sustain. It might be favored by environmentalists, but in fact it does not take the environment seriously enough. As John Gray once put it, our epoch may be one "in which human action is transforming the planet. But it is also one in which the human animal is less than ever in charge. Global warming seems to be in large part the result of the human impact on the planet, but this is not to say humans can stop the process."[3] There are two important ideas in this passage. First, if by the Anthropocene we mean the age when human beings are in charge of their natural environment, we would do well to disabuse ourselves of the notion. Climate change is not an example of how human beings have destroyed the planet. The planet itself will survive unscathed if temperatures on the surface rise 5 or 6 degrees Celsius by 2100, a very modest shift in the context of the Earth's long geological history. Travel 50 million years into our geological past, to the early age of mammals, and the world was roughly 13 degrees Celsius warmer than today. The Arctic was covered with swampy rainforests teeming with reptiles and the seas near the equator may have been as hot as a jacuzzi. There were no human beings, of course, but at least they could not be blamed for the sweltering temperatures or the spectacularly high levels of carbon dioxide in the atmosphere.[4]

It is human beings that might not survive in a similarly ordained future, at least in their current cultural and social form. Yes, we are able to introduce changes in our natural environment and often we lose control over those changes. What that fact teaches us is not that nature has been replaced by human systems but that we are still struggling—and failing—to control natural forces.

The second idea in the quoted passage that I would like to underline is that climate change is no longer a human effect, even if has an anthropogenic origin. The changed climate is now the new natural climate we must live with and adapt to. The Greeks distinguished between different types of causes. Human beings are the efficient cause of climate change. The material cause is to be found in natural processes and our control over them is just as ambiguous as in the case of any other processes.

You could even argue that global warming in its current manifestation is a planetary process. At the beginning of the Eocene epoch 56 million years ago, newly formed magma ignited vast deposits of fossil fuels at the bottom of the oceans, injecting carbon dioxide into the atmosphere and warming the planet by several degrees. In our own time, one of the living creatures inhabiting the planet had a similar impact. In both cases, feedback mechanisms operating over time can be relied upon to maintain a final balance, even if in the latter example the mechanism could well be the destruction of human life. The planet will remain the same.[5]

What does the current pandemic prove? Not, in my opinion, that the major threat to our collective existence now comes from the destructive power of human systems, but that it continues to arise from a dangerous and inhospitable natural environment. Adam Tooze has argued that "what we are living through is the first economic crisis of the Anthropocene."[6] But is this actually the case? Is the threat a direct result of human activity? Nothing about the course of events supports this thesis. The virus struck as viruses have struck since time immemorial: a biological threat taking advantage of the inconvenient fact that we too are part of the biological world. And our response has been what the human response has always been, a sustained effort to escape our mortal coil and build a human world protected from natural threats. Most of us, as the pandemic arrived, did not regard the system of economic growth and capital accumulation as the threat.

Someone once said that it is easier to imagine the end of the world than to imagine the end of capitalism. It is a clever formula, even in its comical effect. And yet, the current crisis proved the opposite. It was much easier to imagine the end of capitalism than to conceive that everything could go on as before. Were we forced to sacrifice countless lives in order to save the machinery of capital accumulation? Not at all. Everyone seemed ready to place the economy on hold in order to save lives, restarting it only when it was safe—or safer—to do so.

The pandemic did not arise from our social and economic systems, just as past pandemics were not the product of feudalism or the "Asiatic mode of production." Disease is of course shaped by human practice and human institutions, but its roots lie much deeper in that mysterious region where nature and culture clash, and have always clashed. Tooze argues that the threat of "emerging infectious diseases" is not a mere accident of nature but the inevitable result of the incorporation of animal life into our food chain. Like the climate crisis, infectious diseases "have anthropogenic drivers." As he puts it, "if we are going to keep huge stocks of domesticated animals and intrude ever more deeply into the last remaining reservoirs of wildlife; if we are going to concentrate in giant cities and travel in ever larger numbers, this comes with viral risks." But what then should the response be? It is revealing that Tooze does not go on to argue that we should respond to the pandemic by reforming social habits and practices. The answer is technological. "If we wish to avoid disasters we should invest in research, in monitoring, in basic public health, in the production and stockpiling of vaccines and essential equipment for our hospitals."

A related argument is that the pandemic is a child of the jet age. There is no doubt that it is, but I do not regard the fact as especially significant. Every human disease will take place within the social and historical context to which it belongs. The Black Death arrived in Europe in October 1347, when twelve ships from the Black Sea docked at the Sicilian port of Messina. Before that, infectious diseases were carried by horse raiders or herds of cattle. The Mongols most likely encountered the plague in the thirteenth century through eating infected marmots. Genghis Khan is described as consuming marmots during his period of exile, and foreign visitors noted the special predilection the Mongols had for consuming rodents. The work of hunting, cooking and tanning marmot hides would have put every hunter, cook, and tanner at risk of infection by *Yersinia pestis*. The long-distance migration of plague strains followed the tracks of Mongol conquest. The Mongols shipped their own grain from Central Asia and Western China to the Middle East, creating ideal conditions for rodents and their fleas to tag along, possibly small rodents which could have played the role of transitional hosts in human outbreaks of plague.[7] But few, I think, would blame it on Mongol technology or Mongol capitalism.

There is nothing particularly distinctive about the current pandemic. Infectious diseases have always resulted from the incorporation of wildlife into our diet, and they have always taken advantage of our life patterns to invade human populations. It should be added that these life patterns and technologies have served both as conduits for spreading the disease and as tools used to fight it. The jet age is also the age of vaccines built on messenger ribonucleic acid.

If the theory that the virus responsible for the pandemic escaped from a lab gains wider acceptance, will it change our fundamental views about the origins of the current disaster? If those such as the respected science journalist Nicholas Wade are correct that this is the most plausible explanation, should one conclude that we live in the Anthropocene or not in the Anthropocene? As Wade argues, the lab theory cannot be ruled out, because virologists have for at least two decades been engaged in a supremely dangerous game. In their laboratories they routinely create viruses more dangerous than those that exist in nature in the belief that by getting ahead of nature they can predict and prevent natural spillovers, the crossover of viruses from an animal host to people.[8] The lab-escape hypothesis would show that our attempts to master nature can also unleash its horrors on the world.

The mastery of nature is an infinitely difficult problem, albeit a problem we cannot run away from. We see that in the way contemporary forms of capitalist organization create the very problems they were meant to address. Meant to push nature away from our daily lives, they have imbricated us all the more deeply with natural forces. In the old days, alders and flowering willows in the Alaskan Arctic stood no taller than a small child. But as temperatures warmed due to fossil fuel emissions and growing seasons lengthened, shrubs started to grow and expand; the alders have fresh buds and the catkins are fuzzing out. Gravel and sandbars that were free of vegetation in old photos now suddenly host verdant shrubs. Today, many of these stand over 6 feet high. Bigger shrubs drew moose, and the process took on a life of its own—quite literally. Species will shift their range as climate conditions change. Some will carry old diseases into human settlements, previously left untouched. In Sweden, lakes and streams previously used for drinking water are now contaminated with the parasite that causes giardiasis, the human intestinal illness. More remarkably still, new hybrid species are appearing, as species brought together by new climate conditions start to interbreed.[9]

At the same time, encroachment on the natural ecosystem and wildlife by agricultural and urban land uses will expose humans and their domestic animals to areas with higher risks and a wider range of vectors. For example, habitat destruction and fragmentation in Cambodia, Thailand, India, Bangladesh and Madagascar brought fruit bats closer to humans and domestic animals, causing outbreaks of Nipah virus infection.[10] Deforestation in Malaysia destroyed the natural habitat of the fruit bats, pushing them out of their ecological niche. Many pig farmers had planted fruit trees around their farms, which attracted the displaced fruit bats. Contaminated fruit fell on the ground and was eaten by the pigs. From the sick pigs the Nipah virus finally hopped onto the human host.

These descriptions—deliberately bucolic—do not evoke cyberpunk scenarios where technology has replaced nature. What they do evoke is the memory of our prehistoric beginnings, where the first human settlements had to struggle to keep nature away. Highly transmissible viral diseases like measles and smallpox entered the human population from domesticated animals. The hunter met his prey only at distance, and when he could touch the prey, the animal was dead. All known transmission mechanisms like sneezing, coughing or diarrhea are not any longer operative in the dead animal, but with the domestication of cattle, sheep and goats, humans were suddenly in close contact with sick animals and zoonotic infections became much more likely. Recent analyses show that the measles virus probably arose together with the appearance of the first large cities in Babylon and China. Smallpox seems to have emerged perhaps 5,000 years ago. One scholar argues that the old founding myth of Europa and the bull—the mother of King Minos of Crete, after whom the continent is named, who was abducted by Zeus in the form of a bull—is really a reference to the domestication of cattle brought to Greece from the Fertile Crescent. The Minotaur is a symbol of the recurrent fear of deadly diseases arising from the mingling of species, chimeras which ate the young children of the earlier inhabitants of Europe. It was too early to know of viruses as their agent, but the famous labyrinth of Minos "might be a type of quarantine imposed on infected subjects."[11]

The link between the climate crisis and disease thus needs to be placed in a broader context. There is no pristine age to which humans can return looking for protection from infectious diseases. All that can be said is that our repeated attempts to escape from the threat of disease have failed. Our links with the natural world run so deep that every attempt to break free has left us exposed to new transmission mechanisms.

The Anthropocene is such an explicitly extravagant concept that it seems to have been developed in order to collapse its own essential meaning: it suggests that human beings are now in control and possession of their natural environment, only to conclude that "we find ourselves each day a bit more entangled in the immense feedback loops of the Earth system."[12] What the present moment shows is that we never left the past, not that a new age is upon us. We never left the frontier. The line between the wilderness and civilization may shift, or it may be sublimated—becoming part of elaborate multivariate computer models rather than a visible line between jungle and settlement—but it is as present today as when human beings started to cultivate the soil and build the first large cities. Our time is not the "human epoch"—as a famous cover of *Nature* called it in 2015—but the epoch of nature.

Was there ever a human epoch?

THE INFINITE GAME

The greatest minds of modern Enlightenment thought—from Bacon and Descartes to John Stuart Mill and even Marx—shared an unshakable belief that human beings would one day become the "masters and possessors of nature." The phrase comes from Descartes, who in many respects deserves to be regarded as the founder of the modern project to remake the world according to a rational plan.

The remarkable thing is how successful the project was. The world was indeed remade. Science has for the first time in human history—science has always existed—been placed in charge of human societies. No serious prophet of the scientific revolution ever promised human beings would get rid of death. Until the branch of modern thought inaugurated by Marx, no one really believed that inequality and labor could be eliminated. As fantastic as the modern project may have sounded when it was first launched, its aspirations were more practical: a life of comfort—free of disease, hunger and fear—where everyone can live to old age and enjoy the pleasures more suited to his or her temperament. The systematic and organized exploitation of natural resources was the suggested way to get there and, until recently, everything seemed to have worked. Large sections of humanity had reached the promised land already; others were catching up fast. To be sure, one still hoped for better treatments for cancer and other diseases—perhaps a cure—and the threat of war never really vanished. Those seemed eminently solvable problems, in no way comparable to past achievements. In a fundamental sense, we had become the possessors of nature, even if there were still some rearguard pockets of resistance to be found.

Within this general psychology, the pandemic was a revealing moment. At first, it was received—as one would expect—with deep tones of skepticism. That disease could again become a societal rather than a purely individual experience was deemed inconceivable. Many in the developed world proceeded to use the only interpretative framework available to them: the epidemic would surely remain confined to the world's backwaters, and no one in Europe or North America had much reason to worry. Later, when this assumption was revealed as a fatal conceit, the shock was made greater by a number of new facts. Not only were developed societies just as vulnerable to infectious disease as the rest of the world, but even their health systems could not be relied upon to work promptly and efficiently. The case of the United States was particularly shocking. We knew, of course, that the healthcare system in America was afflicted with deep and persistent inequalities and lack of access, but for those within the protective perimeter the expectation was that it could deliver the best of modern science and medicine. What we witnessed, instead, was failure at every level of the system.

With the benefit of one more year, the final appraisal is somewhat more nuanced. Countless lives were saved because societies were able to quickly devote resources to fighting the virus and, by developing new vaccines in less than a year, the biomedical community delivered a remarkable scientific success, arguably alongside the greatest medical breakthroughs of modern times. At the same time, it is easy to see that there can be no return to the innocent times before Covid. Too many illusions have been shattered for one to believe again in the final triumph of mind over matter. Revealingly, a report published by Deutsche Bank in December 2020 listed the following as the two top risks to global financial markets in the new year: a virus mutation allowing it to dodge vaccines and serious vaccine side effects. By the beginning of 2021, it became common to speak of a race between immunization and mutation. Tyler Cowen captured the moment:

> Imagine being a leader of a country that has successfully contained Covid, and now realizing that a single mis-

take could undo almost a year of very hard work. You also know that, precisely because your country has been so effective at fighting the virus, it is not on the verge of vaccinating your entire population. What if you let a single returning citizen pass through customs taking one Covid test rather than three? What if you then cannot control the subsequent spread of the strain that person is carrying?[13]

He compared it to being inside a horror movie: just when we think it is safe, the monster comes back, stronger than ever.

There was a fatal flaw with the modern project, even if it escaped detection until very recently. Just as modern science promised the power to control nature, it also moved towards a definition of the universe that made such power ultimately unattainable. Breaking with previous tradition, what the Italian philosopher Giordano Bruno (1548–1600) proposed was an original expansion of the heliocentric planetary system to an infinite and homogeneous universe, where endless planetary systems coexisted, each of them separated from the adjacent ones by a vast extension of space filled with pure air or ether. Unsurprisingly, the theory was regarded with suspicion by his contemporaries. Perhaps they saw the problem.

A century later, when Johannes Kepler came to conceive his universe, it was a modest affair: rigorously finite, with the unique sun star at its center and the immobile stars on the spherical periphery. God is infinite, the creation is not. To which Bruno had responded: the excellence of God is magnified and the greatness of his kingdom made manifest not in one, but in countless suns; not in a single earth, but in an infinity of worlds. Later, when an infinite and homogeneous universe became the scientific norm, the modern project of control was so advanced that no one paid too much attention to the obvious difficulty that an infinite object cannot be mastered. An infinite universe cannot be the object of total and precise knowledge, but only a partial and conjectural one. Astronomy, indeed, is an empirical science. Its field is coextensive with that of observable data. As a science, it has nothing to say about things that are not, and cannot, be seen.[14]

It would be bad enough if by an infinite universe we meant quantitative infinity. But consider qualitative infinity. If there are an unlimited number of kinds of things in nature, no system of scientific laws can ever attain a perfect validity. Every such system works only with a finite number of elements and causes, and thus necessarily leaves out of account other kinds of critical factors...

I would argue that the problem remained relatively marginal and obscure for a long time and only acquired prominence in the twentieth century. We owe that prominence to science fiction. All—or almost all—classics of the genre are reflections on the infinite game of mastery. Infinite, because the object cannot be delimited. Mastery, because the fundamental drive posited by

Bacon or Descartes has not disappeared. Human beings are still forced to struggle for survival in an inhospitable environment.

In *Dune*—the novel by American writer Frank Herbert—the plot centers around the political struggle between two rival families. There are echoes of Shakespeare, remnants of religious scripture and the skulduggery of Roman politics, but that is not what makes *Dune* a masterpiece. What it does that is new and cosmic in scale is turn the planet Arrakis into the protagonist. Even the struggle between House Atreides and House Harkonnen is in the end a sideshow. What matters is the greater struggle between the human mind and those infinite spaces whose mysteries we are summoned to invade. This is no longer the inert nature of Descartes. Dune opens up to the infinite universe of Bruno, never completely known, always revealing new elements and powers, a universe at least as alive as human beings themselves, where the most persistent principles are accident and error.[15] Herbert was critical of that defining trait of Western culture that he called the mathematical attempt to "overcome nature." In *Dune*, the scientist Kynes is someone who "has lived out of rhythm with nature, and he got in the trough of the wave and it tumbled on him."

As Amitav Ghosh puts it in his remarkable *The Great Derangement*, our way of regarding our planet and other interplanetary objects is changing. Our basic understanding about nature is also changing. The illusions of the Enlightenment are crumbling. "The humans of the future will surely understand, knowing what they presumably will know about the history of their forebears on earth, that only in one, very brief era, lasting less than three centuries, did a significant number of their kind believe that planets and asteroids are inert."[16]

There is an image of progress and technology where they are conceived of as a finite game. It is the vision of Descartes and all the other great prophets of the Enlightenment. The goal of technology as a finite game is to bring about a final victory of the human mind over nature and create the conditions for a fully predictable world. When technology is understood as an infinite game, progress is never final—there is no victory—but that fact is welcomed as proof that the human mind must continue to grow in order to face greater and greater challenges. As the writer James Carse argues, a finite game player is trained not only to anticipate every future possibility, but to control the future, to prevent it from altering the past. Infinite game players want to be surprised. Surprise is the very essence of the game. "A finite game is played for the purpose of winning, an infinite game for the purpose of continuing the play."[17]

Whether the conquest of nature is a finite or an infinite game is a question full of consequences for world politics. Remove nature as a perpetual challenge to human life and the international system is suddenly a much simpler one. States are the only sovereign actors.

State competition takes place in a void. Operating in a void, states define themselves by contrast and in opposition to rival powers. The appeal to a higher authority is by definition impossible. In such a system, competition can quickly become unstable because state activity is directed against a rival or rivals rather than a common environment.

If we now reintroduce the external environment into the system, if nature is again an obstacle, state action will be primarily directed towards addressing the challenges emerging from that environment. State competition acquires the nature of a game. What is a game? It is a form of indirect conflict. In a game the players do not directly fight each other. They compete to beat their rivals in a series of operations leading to the successful performance of a task. It is in the nature of a game that the contenders must outperform each other in a task or tasks made difficult by the game environment. In the most developed and perfect game types—the types that better imitate human life—the players share the same environment and must therefore perform against opponents who themselves are trying to complete the same task. Normally, the winner is the player who is able to complete it first or who can complete it a superior number of instances in a given time period.

Where states are engaged in the effort to master an adverse environment, competition takes place against the background of technological power. It is by increasing their control over the external environment that states can increase their power within the system. The reason should be obvious: human power is a variable defined by the extent of our control over natural forces, and power relations closely track the relative success of different actors in obtaining larger and larger measures of control. We could already find a similar thesis in John Locke, whose theory of property and thus of power relations within society ultimately derives from the effort to transform nature: "Whatsoever, then, he removes out of the state that nature hath provided and left it in, he hath mixed his labour with, and joined to it something that is his own, and thereby makes it his property." The transformation to his own ends of things originally found in nature was an activity of human beings connected from the very beginning with their struggle against other human beings: the roughest wedge hewn of flint "was a useful tool, and at the same time a deadly weapon."[18]

Interestingly, the two types of game described above offer very precise images for both the Cold War between the United States and the Soviet Union and the new "world game" between China and the United States. The Cold War was an unconnected game, such as a track race, where the game environment for the players is largely kept separate. In a connected game such as football, the players share the same environment and thus must act against each other in trying to perform their tasks. In his Davos speech in January 2021,

Xi Jinping compared global competition to "a track race, not a wrestling match," but of course it is a wrestling match and that is how China approaches it. The shift from one type of game to the other is due to the rise of a natural environment which the contestants must share. It is because America won the first Cold War—on the premise that the Soviet plan of total political control over the environment is impossible—that a sequel has become impossible.

Placed in circumstances where they have little choice but to increase their power over nature, states are at that very moment committed to the global competition for power. They may come to appreciate the adrenaline rush, a global game offering all the advantages of competition while eliminating, or at least reducing, its risks. The emergence of a dangerous external environment opens up possibilities for state actors to change the global power distribution without the risks arising from direct action against their rivals. Indirect conflict has attractions of its own.

THIS IS HOW YOU WIN THE VIRUS WARS

One of the most striking developments during the early months of the pandemic was the way state competition quickly took over. Always heralded as a textbook case of the need for global cooperation, pandemics turned out to be prime examples of global competition, albeit in the indirect and gamified version described above.

After media outlets built the digital tools helping us compare the outbreaks in different countries, most public discussions started to resemble sports commentary. "How your country compares," as the *Financial Times* put it. Some countries were praised for the way they were able to flatten the curve. Others seemed to compete only to avoid being last. There were long debates about the most appropriate metrics to evaluate relative performance, and elaborate explanations of why some excelled while others failed. For a while, Sweden seemed to be a winner. Months later it was declared a loser. Germany went from exceptional to average, but New Zealand kept surpassing itself, announcing by the end of the year that it was now reaching the benchmark for coronavirus elimination. One newspaper wrote about Italy, in lines meant to evoke a story worthy of the Olympics:

> More importantly, Italy showed the rest of Europe how to turn things around. Spooked by the dramatic death toll in the Lombardy region, the government of Prime Minister Giuseppe Conte sprang into action, using the license he won through emergency decrees to get the country's famously sclerotic administration moving. That helped Italy flatten the curve more quickly than anyone thought possible.[19]

Morbid league tables multiplied. They were criticized, of course, but most often because the picture they offered was too static to reflect the realities of the ongoing competition.

With the arrival of the vaccines, state competition took a new form, but not a milder one: an ugly global race for enough vaccine doses where the losers are denied a path out of the pandemic. Suddenly, the laggards from the previous iteration of the game seemed for the first time to be ahead. The United Kingdom was the first jurisdiction to approve a Covid vaccine and quickly pulled ahead of other large, advanced economies in the race to vaccinate its population: a rare pandemic success for the country. The United States followed, with the European Union falling behind. In December 2020, in just two weeks, Israel succeeded in vaccinating close to 20% of its citizens, leading the world by a very large measure and drawing on its origins as a tightly knit small nation fighting for survival. Prime Minister Netanyahu was recorded in January telling a closed-door meeting that the pandemic had been vanquished and raising the claim for Israel as the first country to do it. "You all understand that everything we are talking about the corona is just compensation for the past. It's over," Netanyahu told members of a protest group representing independent business owners.[20] In April 2021, experts in Britain announced the country was no longer in a pandemic, as data showed the vaccination program was reducing symptomatic Covid infections by up to 90%. Sarah Walker, an epidemiologist at Oxford, said the country had moved from a pandemic to an endemic situation, where the virus circulates at a low and largely controllable level.

There were also those such as Russia or China who continued to bet on their own vaccines, and despite concerns over incomplete trial data and the domestic approval processes, the market demand was strong, as many parts of the world simply have no access to the vaccines developed in Europe and the United States. By March, both the Gamaleya and Sinopharm vaccines were slowly becoming the two dominant choices for many countries in Southeast Asia and Latin America. Vaccines gained Russia and China goodwill and recognition from populations eager to see some light at the end of the pandemic. More obviously, it was good business, and the kind capable of opening up new doors in the future. In some cases, vaccines may even have been traded for concrete political benefits. Although never officially confirmed, credible reports suggest China may have offered countries such as Paraguay and Brazil access to its vaccines if they changed their position on Taiwan and Huawei, respectively.[21] The United States, India, Japan and Australia responded with a new vaccine partnership during the first Quad virtual summit in March 2020. In parts of Asia, countries could afford to wait and see because the infection had been decisively contained within their borders. Finally, there were those in the developing world who seemed to have dropped out of the vaccine wars altogether.

India, a pharmaceutical giant, used the opportunity to affirm itself as a global player. Under the massive Vaccine

Maitri program, India exported more than 66 million doses of vaccines to ninety-five countries worldwide in the first few months of 2021. Of these about 10 million were grants from the government, 20 million were sent as part of the global COVAX facility and the remaining 36 million were commercial exports. As Raja Mohan put it, vaccines add "to the good side of the ledger for India: that India is there, and that it has capabilities."[22] Tragically, the effort did not go according to plan. Just as Delhi was selling and giving away vaccines in order to gain friends and to influence countries, the devastating second wave of Covid hit the country harder than perhaps any other country had been hit. Vaccine exports were frozen, and India was suddenly forced to ask the United States to lift its own export limits for critical raw materials. Production lines in India would soon grind to a halt without access to thirty-seven critical items, including filters, plastic tubes and raw goods. Without access to the large Indian manufacturing base, countries in Africa and elsewhere were suddenly left stranded. Covid came at a time when India's standing in its neighborhood was already shrinking. The pandemic will make it more difficult for the country to compete with China in a region hungry for development assistance and economic growth.

Writing in January 2021, Duncan Robinson of *The Economist* urged the European Union to abandon the fatal illusion "that rolling out the vaccine is not a competition at all." A vaccination race is the perfect place to exercise your competitive spirit: "If a group including some of the world's most successful societies cannot vaccinate their populations swiftly, then any pretensions that the EU is a potential superpower look ridiculous."[23] It quickly got worse. When the European Union received a string of bad news about interrupted or reduced supplies from both Pfizer and AstraZeneca, it responded by threatening to block vaccine exports across the English Channel. This was the perfect background for the intense competition between the two jurisdictions that Brexit had set up in advance. On 29 January, a febrile day in European politics, Brussels put forward a legal mechanism requiring that vaccine exports be subject to an authorization by the EU's member states.

Without the production of a valid authorization, the export of such goods would be banned. The instrument stated that it was "not the intention of the Union to restrict exports any more than absolutely necessary," a stirring admission that it could in fact be used to stop the flow of vaccine doses to the United Kingdom. More damagingly, the measure was intended to win a political or even an intellectual dispute, but it promised little in terms of actually delivering more vaccine doses to citizens. It was surprising to see such a carnivorous approach from a political bloc that detests carnivorous behavior, an admission that vaccination was indeed a competitive game, but one leading directly to the conclusion that a more forceful approach should have been adopted much earlier.

At the end of March, and at the request of the European Commission, Italian military police entered a vaccine plant and seized the notable amount of 29 million vaccine doses. Several European officials and politicians rushed to celebrate the coup, which promised to vindicate the new strategy and offer renewed hopes of a boost in supplies. Unfortunately, as the Italian police eventually admitted, the doses were ready for shipment not to Britain but to Belgium. Soon after, following a video meeting of the European Council, the Commission President seemed to announce that an export ban on AstraZeneca vaccines had been imposed, even if she left some room for the company to move first. "I think it is clear for the company that, first of all the company has to catch up, has to honour the contract it has with the European member states, before it can engage again in exporting vaccines," Ursula von der Leyen said.[24] Britain started working on plans to accelerate the onshoring of vaccine production and prevent the risk that decisions made elsewhere could disrupt a successful campaign.

There is a lot that went wrong with the European Commission's vaccination strategy. But before everything else, there was complacency. Back in the summer of 2020, the predominant feeling in Brussels and many European capitals was that the virus could be controlled through savvy policy measures. The contrast with the health calamity in the United States made European officials forget that the pandemic was, in fact, a state of emergency requiring a decisive approach to vaccination. Instead, most believed that vaccines would eventually be needed to extirpate the virus, but the process could be conducted against the background of a waning pandemic, at least in Europe. There was no urgency in signing the necessary contracts with the most promising manufacturers, with protracted haggling over prices further delaying the process.

We now know that time was of critical importance, and that the sooner procedures could be tested and perfected, the sooner a high yield of vaccine doses could be expected. The lack of urgency was also reflected in the attempt to bring a number of exogenous considerations into the process. For many months the European Union seemed more interested in scoring political points on solidarity, market power and negotiating clout than in focusing laser-like on the task at hand: getting as many vaccines as fast as possible into the arms of its citizens. It was easy to see all these problems coming. They were like bad omens and they kept piling up.

The vaccine wars are an instance of the broader genus of technology wars. The reason one could easily guess that the European Union would struggle to find its footing is that the bloc has a long-standing problem with technology, seeing it more as a threat than an imperative. And it misses the fundamental nature of the imperative.

First, advanced technology is by definition scarce and competitive. It cannot be normalized: there is always a better way to obtain the same outcome through superior methods. The pandemic was a great teacher in this respect, showing that technology can always move faster and achieve more, or that we are chasing a moving frontier—but the lesson is applicable to normal times as well. During a pandemic, it makes a vital difference whether vaccines are available now or in two months' time, both in terms of saving lives and resuscitating the economy.

This was never understood in Brussels, with the Commission insisting it had secured billions of doses but forgetting to consider *when* these doses would be available. Even in normal times, being able to lead in key technological areas will sooner or later be translated into more visible forms of global power.

Second, the European Union as a whole—its officials, politicians and organic intellectuals—seems unable to understand that technology is political. You cannot keep it out of politics, and this means that politics must adjust to technology at least as much and probably more than technology must adjust to politics. There is no way to be a technological leader without taking risky decisions, without embracing the possibility of failure and without being generous with money and rules—two higher divinities the European Commission will never desecrate. It is revealing that, while Britain placed a venture capitalist at the head of its vaccine program, the European Union opted for a trade negotiator. It was a puzzling choice. What does vaccine procurement have to do with the creation of legal rules?

Or consider how the British Health Secretary Matt Hancock was impressed by the end of the movie *Contagion*, in which there are not enough vaccines for everyone and they have to be awarded by a lottery. One advisor told Sky: "He was always really aware from the very start, first that the vaccine was really important, second that when a vaccine was developed we would see an almighty global scramble for this thing."[25] You may smile, but whether it comes from movies or scientific papers, a "technological imagination" is the necessary beginning of good policy today. As French President Macron expressed it in a television interview in March, European leaders had failed to see that vaccines could be developed as soon as they were, and this is why the European Union as a whole fell behind. "We didn't shoot for the stars. That should be a lesson for all of us. We were wrong to lack ambition, to lack the madness, I would say, to say: It's possible, let's do it," Macron said. He compared the outcome to that across the Atlantic: "We didn't think it would happen that quickly... You can give that to the Americans, as early as the summer of 2020 they said: let's pull out all the stops and do it."[26]

A NEW SYSTEM

To me, it seemed that the pandemic was throwing light on the structure of the international system. World politics is going through a remarkable transformation.

Conflict between great powers is back with a vengeance. Trade disputes have grown into trade wars with no end in sight. Technology has become a battlefield between states, afraid of falling behind in the race to control powerful new tools such as artificial intelligence. China is daily increasing its reach into some of the most critical transport and communication networks, but the United States has fought back by excluding Chinese companies from global value chains under its control. The coronavirus outbreak quickly became a battleground for geopolitical competition, with China openly attempting to use the moment of strategic opportunity to shift global power relations.

The world we live in is no longer that announced by the dreams of a liberal international society following the collapse of the Soviet Union and the Chinese growth miracle. And yet, if international conflict has made a comeback, its impact so far has been limited. Global trade has not collapsed, multinational companies continue to invest and operate across borders and—before the pandemic—citizens enjoyed growing access to international travel. During the outbreak, scientists and universities from different countries worked together on research and technological innovation. Some global organizations and institutions seem weakened, but others have been created or expanded. The global media and information space has only deepened as a result of Covid.

Increasingly we seem to live in a world neither at war nor at peace. Conflict takes place below the threshold of kinetic war or other forms of direct confrontation, but is no less intense because of that. A number of authors have tried to find an idea capable of capturing this predicament and making it easier to understand, but so far no plausible alternative has been offered. Hybrid war seems to refer to the combination of kinetic and other forms of conflict such as propaganda or sabotage. It may have been a useful concept by which to describe events in the Crimea before Russia annexed the peninsula, but it offers little in the case of the ongoing trade war between China and the United States, or the intense competition to come out of the pandemic in better shape than all direct rivals. Nor can the concept of hybrid war be considered as in any way new. Every past war has included nonmilitary strategies and tactics.

What has been noted with greater precision is that contemporary forms of conflict seem to go together with globalization and interdependence. I noted in *The Dawn of Eurasia* how the use—and abuse—of information can now take advantage of the internet and open new fronts of conflict, as in the case of cyber-attacks or hacking into information systems to collect and disseminate information. Other tactics include the purchase of infrastructure in other states, the corruption or blackmail of foreign officials and the manipulation of energy flows or energy prices, all of them magnified in an integrated global economy.

The coronavirus crisis is arguably the first truly global crisis. Everyone is in this together, experiencing the same fears and emotions, not merely watching the same events. And yet we are each responding to the crisis in our own way. Global cooperation is entirely missing. Worse, the political dynamics have set up a great contest where each nation or group of nations adopts its preferred approach to stopping the infection and restarting the economy, taking the enormous gamble that it will prove superior to the alternatives being pursued elsewhere. It is a deadly gamble. Many of these distinctive approaches have failed and are failing, with tragic consequences. If this is a drama, we are still far from reaching the final act.

The concept of a game—the world game—seems to me a particularly apt way to explain conflict in a connected world. There is, first, the fact that conflict is kept below a certain threshold of destructiveness. A game can be bloody and destructive, but competitors are supposed to stay within certain limits, at least for the duration of the game.

Second, in a game the competitors or opponents are inextricably linked together. They are brought together in the same space and their goals and actions have been defined in such a way that they encroach or impinge on each other. They act in the same generalized environment. This is increasingly the case for state actors today. They are so dependent on each other and so tightly connected as links in global networks that they cannot but feel vulnerable, and may not resist the temptation to move first in order to avoid or minimize the consequences of what others decide to do. This is the main and most lasting consequence of the coronavirus pandemic. It has inaugurated a world of cutthroat competition for valuable resources, where disaster lurks and where citizens must rely on their states for security and prosperity.

Finally, the world political and economic system resembles the dynamics of a game in a critical, often overlooked, aspect. In a game you never fight your opponent directly. There are moves and relations that tie you together and you fight your opponent by using those moves and relations against him. Even two boxers are not trying to punch each other like two brawlers on the street: they are acting within a predefined contest and thinking about the fight as a whole and about the best strategy to bring about victory, which is something different from destroying your opponent. Those who make it personal are more likely to lose. The players have learned over years or decades how to master and perfect all the possibilities opened by the game. They use the possibilities of the game to beat their opponent.

The same happens with technology today, which operates at the level of the system itself. Using the power of the global technological system to pursue your aims is much more effective than using more direct means. When I submitted above that this is an exceedingly complex game, I had in mind the process by which an actor comes to master the way technology works, with interconnected parts and knock-on effects. It is almost indistinguishable from the process by which one learns how to play a game.

As many have argued, games have always been metaphors for warfare. The team sports are rambling charges in which attackers and defenders, led by their captains, ebb and flow up and down the battlefield in a clash of will and power. Tennis is a pistol duel. Running races are breakneck chases between predator and prey.[27] Now the metaphor has become real, more real than reality itself.

As the global system of exchange comes increasingly to depend on flows of data and information, the game is less a sports game and more a computer or video game. No strategy can ignore the fact that states now operate within a global system that has been considerably automated and seems increasingly able to dictate outcomes, rewarding or punishing those agents that fail to understand how it all works. Think of the rhythm of financial crisis, global investment, and economic incentives. Human beings have of course built this system. We built the world game, and we are the ones playing it.

THE RETURN OF GEOPOLITICS

Uri Friedman has argued that every geopolitical age has its own form of national power. The era ushered in by Covid-19 is no exception, revealing the importance of what Friedman calls resilient power: "a country's capacity to absorb systemic shocks, adapt to these disruptions, and quickly bounce back from them."[28]

Previous ages placed a premium on different forms of national power. I find it revealing that for a number of decades these were directly connected to the "system of states." After the Cold War, soft power. The suggestion here was that a stable and open global system would be governed by the free flow of money and ideas, not so differently from how democratic societies govern themselves. Even during the Cold War, national power was directed against other states and aimed at maintaining stability through nuclear weapons and alliance networks. One has to return to early modern Europe to find a system of power firmly anchored in the attempt to control an adverse natural environment through new transport and industrial technologies aimed at the acquisition of territory or geography, including, of course, colonial possessions. Friedman notes that the reason a country such as Australia performed better during the current pandemic than most of its Western peers may well have been because of its history of dealing with natural disasters and reacting to new and unexpected circumstances in a context of adversity.

The history of the changes I am tracing is well contained in the history of the term "geopolitics." When the term was coined at the beginning of the twentieth century, it was meant to capture the struggle or competition between states for the effective control over territory.

The notion of an external environment was obviously part of the concept, but geography or territory were seen as passive objects of state action and jealousy. Later, other sources of state power started to be regarded as more central than having control over a large territory: population, industrial prowess, the economy, knowledge and culture. In our time, the use of the term "geopolitics" is often perplexing. It has retained the element of state competition, but it no longer refers to geography or territory, making one wonder what the prefix "geo" is doing there.

One of the lessons of the pandemic is that geopolitics is back, not in the amputated sense of state competition but in the original sense of seeing the sources of state power as directly related to the ability to control the external environment, which has nonetheless become much more active and threatening and can no longer be equated with mere territory. Geopolitics today refers to the power of nature, the influence of the "earth system."

In 1925, Karl Haushofer wrote: "This prefix means much and demands much. It relates politics to the soil. It rids politics of arid theories and senseless phrases which might trap our political leaders into hopeless Utopias. It puts them back on solid ground."[29] He presented geopolitics as an "exact science," a promise that remained undelivered. The prefix "geo" may have been intended as a constraint on power, but restricted to its geographical meaning, the result was rather the opposite: a vortex of state control in search of unlimited "living space," which is how the Nazis read Haushofer. Today, the prefix can play a more salutary role, alerting us to the limitations of human power, and turning states away from direct competition and towards the urgent task of survival in increasingly adverse conditions. Geopolitics has become a technological imperative.

In order to understand how unusual the current moment truly is, keep in mind that for centuries we have firmly professed a belief in what I call a "system of states." Metaphorically, this is a room without a roof. Nothing stands above the multiple nation states. There are differences of power between them, to be sure, but they still exist and operate at the same level, since no overarching actor can be found above them. It is necessary to return to the High Middle Ages to find a different architecture. Take the reign of Pope Innocent III. How did the "system of states" look in 1215? In Europe, or more broadly speaking in Christendom, the Pope stood as the feudal ruler of a great many countries or realms. As the general "speculator"—the supervisor set over nations by Christ himself—he was entitled to depose princes, release subjects from their oaths of allegiance, confer crowns by making kings and dispose of territories. To medieval jurists no other conception would have seemed acceptable. How could you bring order to the political world if no power stood above the warring states? As a matter of fact, modern politics has not been impervious to this demand. We have continued to look for a "speculator," whether the candidate was to be found in the forces of global finance or the bureaucratic apparatus of the United Nations. European countries have in fact developed a viable supervisor, whose seat in Brussels cannot but remind us of the glory that was the Holy See.

The pandemic, however, signaled a change. If power is understood as the ability to change and shape social reality, then the virus quickly revealed itself as the new supervisor. All policies were quickly measured and evaluated according to their ability to stop the spread of infection, and a number of dramatic changes to the way we live were imposed with little or no democratic deliberation, as if the final arbiter to which one must appeal had been transferred from the people or the general will to nature or the natural environment, of which the virus stood as representative. Even the most radical political movement could never have dreamt of what the pandemic brought about: a radical and uncontested change to collective life. And yet, state after state gladly submitted to the unannounced guest, not only as a brute force but as the arbiter of their actions and decisions, the judge to whom one appealed when determining failure and success. It felt like the return of a supernatural agent, not because there is anything supernatural about a virus, but because its political power differed so dramatically from that inert and docile element we used to call "nature." All this from a collection of virus particles, spread all over the world, which combined together would fit inside a soft drinks can.[30]

The new ruler over all lands, the virus!

GEOPOLITICS OF CLIMATE

In a book published just a few short months after the Covid-19 outbreak, the academic and climate activist Andreas Malm raised a stimulating question: "Why did the states of the global North act on corona but not on climate?"[31] After the virus outbreak, measures were imposed to confine citizens to their homes, while a distinction was promptly laid down between essential and nonessential economic activities. Harrods in London, which stayed open throughout the Blitz, actually closed on March 20, 2020. Car manufacturers switched off their assembly lines and some even turned to producing ventilators. As Malm wryly notes, a principle never before contemplated was suddenly put into practice: "Some forms of production and commerce meet basic human needs, while others have no legitimate claims to uninterrupted revenue streams and can be discontinued forthwith."

On climate, the policy response has been considerably more subdued. Why the difference? I agree that there is a difference, but much depends on how we interpret it. Malm rules out a number of explanations for the disparity. He does not agree, for example, that the pandemic is a greater and more urgent threat, quoting figures showing that we may already be facing 150,000 annual deaths from climate change. He was writing in the first summer of the pandemic. Since then, those who warned about its tragic costs were proven right. By the summer of 2021, at least 4 million people had died, a number certain to vastly undercount the real death toll. An analysis published in May 2021 raised the figure to 6.9 million deaths worldwide.[32] In the same month, *The Economist* suggested as a central estimate, that 10 million people might already have died. As the pandemic continues to rage in highly populous regions, and as the inadequacy of the official tally is further exposed, it cannot be excluded that we will arrive at a final death count of 20 million or more. Imagine if nothing had been done.

Notwithstanding these obvious facts, Malm thinks it all comes down to the identity of the victims. The pandemic actually struck distinct members of the dominant class and the populations of advanced capitalist countries as its first victims. Climate is still, for now, primarily a problem for the other half of the planet. Could this be the explanation? Suppression of the virus fits much better with political patterns. It could be pursued by national states, even with nationalist motives, while emission cuts to save the planet would benefit the whole world and bring about a new concept of humanity as a collective actor.

There is another reason that Malm ignores. With the pandemic, it is possible to imagine that this is a war we can win, and win decisively. The total mobilization we witnessed throughout the first year of the pandemic was possible because everyone interpreted it as a temporary effort, after which things could be expected to return to normal, even if normal here most likely means a new normal. With climate change, the revolution in social and economic life that we all hear is necessary is meant to be more or less permanent. It is hardly surprising that states and societies are still hesitant, or that they doubt their abilities to take the leap.

There is no reason to believe that the geopolitics of climate change will break with the national model criticized by climate activists. That emergency, when it becomes unavoidable, will be addressed by national states against the same background of rivalry or competition. As U.S. Secretary of State Antony Blinken put it in April, ahead of a White House virtual climate summit, "it is difficult to imagine the United States winning the long-term strategic competition with China if we cannot lead the renewable energy revolution." The contrast with the pandemic is merely this: that the battle against climate change will not be over in two or three years. The climate is forever.

It is helpful to think of adaptation as the climate equivalent of virus containment and decarbonization as the equivalent of vaccination. If it was possible to compress the long and difficult process of vaccine development into less than a year, perhaps something similar could be attempted for energy and transport infrastructure. But what we saw during the pandemic, and what perhaps shocked many of us, was how countries took a remorselessly egotistic approach to containment. They willingly embraced the logic of a race against every other country, and if the race demanded that others must lose, so be it. In the early stages of the pandemic, for example, masks and ventilators were hoarded by those who could afford to do so.

It is natural, therefore, to expect something similar during the long climate crisis. Heat waves can be mitigated with more widespread use of air conditioning, while remote work will eliminate the need for stressful commutes and landscaping can keep cities livable, for those who can afford these remedial measures. With sea level rise, some coastlines will be abandoned, but cities and countries may also decide to build defensive infrastructure. Staten Island in New York is planning a US$615 million seawall to withstand a 300-year storm. The plan consists of a series of levees, berms and seawalls stretching 5.3 miles from Staten Island's eastern shore neighborhoods of Fort Wadsworth to Great Kills. In December 2020, the Chinese State Council issued a circular laying out measures for the quality development of weather modification. According to the document, China will have a developed weather modification system by 2025, with breakthroughs in fundamental research in key technologies.

The logic of adaptation follows the pattern we saw during the pandemic, with countries investing in testing and hospital facilities, and trusting their own policy decisions more than any global approach. In an emergency, the temptation is to focus on measures whose benefits do not extend to other actors: excludable goods where incentives are better aligned. Shocking as it may sound, some countries may even expect to benefit from the chaos. If only some cities have the material resources and political organization to limit the impact of climate change, companies and skilled labor might flow there.

At four degrees of warming, corn yields in the United States are expected to drop by almost half. China, Argentina or Brazil could lose at least a fifth of their productivity. Contrary to popular expectations, it is not easy to move croplands poleward a few hundred miles. "Yields in places like remote areas of Canada and Russia, even if they warmed by a few degrees, would be limited by the quality of the soil there, since it takes many centuries for the planet to produce optimally fertile dirt."[33] This should be enough to make us rethink the notion that countries such as Russia will come out of the shock as winners—the idea that thawing permafrost will be replaced by verdant croplands is laughable—but the geopolitical point is not lost. We do not know at present if four degrees is a plausible scenario for the end of the century, but great powers such as China or the United States should take the possibility seriously. Suddenly, access to croplands becomes a matter of national security and control of strategic territory may once again become an index of national power.

Perhaps Siberia will be transformed into farmed land after all, but that will have to take place with heavy investment, which naturally can come only from China. And it is not just croplands, of course: many critical segments in global supply chains, from semiconductors to rare earths, are concentrated in regions highly vulnerable to climate risk. At best, major powers will want to develop global networks of economic and political influence allowing them to guarantee access to vital supplies even in the most adverse scenarios. China is doing this through its "dual circulation" strategy and the quickly expanding Belt and Road initiative. Market mechanisms are decidedly insufficient in a world where a critical port may suddenly be flooded, or a vital supplier of agricultural imports engulfed by fires.

In theory, states could become so captured by a collective action problem that they would never be able to move beyond adaptation. Global climate policy imposes concentrated costs on early movers who, nevertheless, only capture a small fraction of the benefits. In dealing with the consequences of climate change, by contrast, cost and benefit are aligned. Collective action models have an iron logic, but the evidence does not seem to support their predictions, as a recent study documents, and several mechanisms explain why it would always be implausible.[34] An increasingly committed public will call for a more structural approach to the climate crisis, and in democracies the public will sooner or later shape policy. At the very least, by closing off the path of business as usual, collective consciousness ensures that technological innovation and business investment take place in other directions. And if a country becomes a leader in decarbonization, it will hardly be confined to the role of Good Samaritan. Because the solution is inevitably technological, it can profit by finding other countries interested in acquiring it. We saw that in the case of the global market for vaccines. The incentives are the reverse of what many economists have predicted. If everyone will eventually have to move to a sustainable solution, you can corner the market by moving first.

Forget about the climate crisis as a moment to overcome geopolitics. More likely, geopolitics will be more present than ever. There is a lot of attention in the public debate to the increased efficiency of solar panels or wind turbines, but these technologies have their own industrial chains. Copper, nickel, cobalt, chromium and other critical minerals will be required in much larger quantities for decarbonization. The most important rich metal deposits tend to be in politically and socially unstable places. As John Dizard notes, "for Europeans, the energy transformations will almost certainly require a much larger industrial and social spending commitment to Africa."[35] As for the hydrogen economy, it will be far more dependent on platinum from southern Africa than the oil industry ever was on the Gulf deposits. In September 2020, the European Commission warned member states that shortages of elements used to make batteries and renewable energy equipment threatened the European Union's climate goals, while exposing the bloc to supply squeezes by China, which dominates the processing of strontium and lithium before they go into magnets and batteries for electric vehicles. For lithium, almost all the supply from Australia is processed in China. One possible strategy is to use the Copernicus Earth observation satellite "to find new resources and manage existing ones."[36] The whole discussion takes us back a century to when national power was measured in territorial deposits of raw materials.

There will be fights for new resources, with demand for the materials in solar panels tripling or more over the next few decades, and the need for battery ingredients like cobalt, lithium and other rare earths growing so quickly that countries will be forced to scramble for control over specific geographies. "That is, mines all around the world opened to disgorge resources at a rate much faster than those that powered the global industrial revolution over centuries, and in ways that invariably generate state conflict"[37] If the climate crisis will inaugurate a new economic and technological model, the last thing we should expect is that the transition will be a peaceful one. What history teaches us is that moments of transition are understood by state actors as a threat and an opportunity, rare moments when new orders may be created and new states may ascend to the commanding heights. It was by leading the fossil fuel revolution that England became the ruler of a global empire, and the United States took advantage of a similar opportunity by leading the technological transformations of the Second Industrial Revolution.

In September 2020, Xi Jinping announced a plan to achieve carbon neutrality before 2060. If China were to achieve its announced goal, it would lower global warming projections by around 0.2 to 0.3 degrees Celsius, the biggest single reduction ever estimated by the Climate Action Tracker (CAT). Assuming full implementation of the Paris "pledges and targets," without the new China announcement, CAT estimates the global temperature increase will be 2.7 degrees Celsius by 2100. The Chinese announcement would lower it to around 2.4 to 2.5 degrees Celsius.

Traditionally, of course, it is the capacity to mobilize resources that stands as a marker of national power. How was it possible that a country so obsessively committed to the goal of national rejuvenation was now announcing what Pierre Charbonnier calls a "program of fossil disarmament"?[38] If we knew something about China and climate, it was surely that the country has long held that wealthier nations, who benefited from earlier industrialization, should carry most of the economic burden for preventing catastrophic warming. In 2008, an article by Zhai Yong from the Environment and Resource Protection Committee of the National People's Congress, argued that an increasing number of Western countries were politicizing the climate issue to contain China's economic and political rise. Today, Elon Musk and Tesla are receiving the same red-carpet treatment that Beijing gave to senior executives of the old fossil economy two decades ago.[39] What changed?

The answer is that China is not so much announcing a retreat from a technological model as the beginning of a new one. The country leads the world in clean energy investment, with its current level of investment in climate change being approximately equal to that of the United States and the European Union combined. A lot is at stake. As each economic bloc increasingly focuses on specific technologies, it must make sure that those technologies become dominant, providing something of a global standard. The European Union has actively bet on hydrogen. The European Green Deal could have a major impact on Russia, a country heavily dependent on exports of fossil fuels to the European Union. Wood Mackenzie, a respected energy consultancy, now has a scenario where oil prices could fall to US$10 per barrel by 2050 if the world accelerates the transition to clean energy. The year 2025 could become an inflection point for the critical automobile industry, the moment when electric and combustion vehicles are projected to cost the same. Countries in East Asia are racing to develop the battery technology of the future, and China is developing integrated supply chains for electric cars in Indonesia. European companies are still world leaders in wind turbines and Germany is striving for global leadership in hydrogen technology, while China threatens to quickly catch up even in these areas. Where China is still lagging, one perceptive report notes, is in "breakthrough innovation that can alter entire markets and create paradigm shifts."[40]

Initial estimates suggest that the pledge made by China in September 2020 to go carbon neutral could involve a total investment of up to US$15 trillion. If even a small fraction of that amount is invested in transformative clean energy technologies like fusion power, it could mean Chinese firms would be more likely to own the intellectual property that powers the planet at the end of this century.[41] The goal is to control as many of the key technologies powering the climate economy as possible. No country can expect to lead the process without a firm commitment to decarbonize. "Just as the advent of coal and oil remade the world, clean energy is set to do the same. The energy transition will not only cut emissions: it will redistribute power."[42] The fact that China has continued to invest in coal power—the country built over three times as much coal plant capacity as the rest of the world in 2020—may seem at odds with its bold climate goals, but the contradiction disappears once we understand that what Chinese authorities envision is a diverse industrial base, where investment in emerging technologies can go together with less advanced sectors for as long as those remain marginally profitable. Rising concern for energy security provides a strong rationale for allowing some coal capacity expansion, and restricting the growth of coal is far more of a political challenge than expanding renewables.[43]

There is something I would call a "technological order" which is deeper and more fundamental than political and economic orders, albeit less visible and often taken for the way nature presents itself. The last time we witnessed a change in the "technological order" was with the industrial revolutions of the modern age. The climate crisis signals a similar change, the moment when our fundamental way of relating to the natural environment is rethought and, as a result, new political and economic arrangements become both possible and necessary.

WELCOME TO THE END TIME

In his 2014 novel, *The Peripheral*, William Gibson develops the striking new concept of the Jackpot. Ironically named, it expresses the moment when everything suddenly goes wrong at the same time. He sees it as environmental exhaustion. Human beings have an obvious tendency to use all the available resources around them. As one specific supply is used up, they turn elsewhere.

These supplies may be to some extent fungible, so it is possible to disguise the disappearance of one source by using more of the remaining ones. Inevitably it all comes to an end, as complete environmental depletion suddenly reveals itself. "More a climate than an event, so not the way apocalypse stories liked to have a big event, after which everybody ran around with guns, looking like Burton and his posse, or else were eaten alive by something caused by the big event. Not like that." Here is how Gibson describes it:

> Droughts, water shortages, crop failures, honeybees gone like they almost were now, collapse of other keystone species, every last alpha predator gone, antibiotics doing even less than they already did, diseases that were never quite the one big pandemic but big enough to be historic events in themselves.[44]

For a while it seemed that the coronavirus pandemic could at least produce a drop in carbon dioxide emissions. It did. Emissions declined by around 7% in 2020, the equivalent to all the carbon emissions India produces in a normal year.[45] They quickly recovered, however. By December, energy-related emissions were 2% higher than they were in the same month a year earlier.[46] Ironically, the pandemic has made global warming even worse, because the reduction in air pollution meant there were fewer particles in the air: soot and sulphate particles from car exhaust and burning coal help cool the planet by reflecting light back into space. Overall, the planet was about 0.03 degrees Celsius warmer for the year because the air had fewer cooling aerosols.[47] Measurements from the Mauna Loa Observatory in Hawaii in March show that 2021 is expected to be the first year on record that sees carbon dioxide in the atmosphere reach levels 50% higher than the preindustrial baseline for longer than a few days.[48] In April 2021, the National Oceanic and Atmospheric Administration reported that the global average of atmospheric carbon dioxide hit 412.5 parts per million in 2020, the highest level in 3.6 million years.

The first year of the pandemic was also a notable year in the history of the climate crisis. The International Federation of Red Cross and Red Crescent Societies thinks that about 10 million people were displaced by climate events such as floods and droughts in the six-month period from September 2020 to February 2021. The 2020 Atlantic hurricane season had thirty named storms, the most in recorded history. The very active 2005 season, which included Hurricane Katrina, only had twenty-eight. In California, out of the six biggest wildfires in state history, five occurred in 2020. In Texas, natural gas-fired plants, utility-scale wind power and coal plants tripped offline due to the extreme cold weather brought by a winter storm in early 2021. Throughout 2020, locusts swarmed in unprecedented numbers in dozens of countries from Kenya to Pakistan, as a result of unusually prolonged rains. Wildfires blazed along the Arctic Circle in the summer, incinerating tundra and permafrost zones amid exceptionally high temperatures. The temperature in Verkhoyansk in Russia, north of the Arctic Circle, rose to 38 degrees Celsius in June. It was warmer there than it has ever been, on any June day, in the entire recorded history of Miami.[49] A year later, at the end of June 2021, temperatures in British Columbia, Canada, reached a shocking 47.9 degrees Celsius. The lightning from the dry thunderstorms that developed was so intense that over 700,000 lightning flashes were recorded in 15 hours. In a world without climate change, these would be the kind of anomalies that would happen once in 100,000 years. We are entering a world that has little or nothing in common with the "climate niche" of the last 11,000 years, the temperate Holocene, corresponding with the development of agriculture, writing systems, urban living and art. Human civilization, in short.

We are in a way back at the beginning, faced with a hostile environment and not at all sure how to make it serve our interests. On second thoughts, it is hardly surprising that the current moment feels like a beginning. For the first time, our environment encompasses the whole planet and our technology must strive for a planetary order. Past successes were limited to local circumstances and cannot easily be replicated on a higher plane. It may feel like the end time, when things cannot continue as before and the very survival of the species is suddenly at stake. The end of a world; but every end contains a new beginning.

NOTES

1. SPACESHIP EARTH

1. Jane Smith, "Inside the Covid Ward," UnHerd, January 6, 2021.
2. Noah Smith, "Imagine the Covid-19 Economy Before Zoom and Amazon," Bloomberg, March 7, 2021.
3. Leila Abboud, "Drinks maker Moët Hennessy predicts liquor 'renaissance'," *Financial Times*, May 12, 2021.
4. Alexandre Tanzi and Michael Sasso, "Affluent Americans Rush to Retire in New 'Life-Is-Short' Mindset," Bloomberg, April 30, 2021.
5. R. Buckminster Fuller, *Operating Manual for Spaceship Earth* (Lars Müller, 2008), 57.
6. Steve Rose, "Eight go mad in Arizona: how a lockdown experiment went horribly wrong," *Guardian*, July 13, 2020.
7. Katie Warren, "Singapore built the world's first bubble facility so people can travel for business without having to quarantine—and it's in an expo center. We got a sneak peak of the rooms, facilities, and food," Insider, March 5, 2021.
8. Carl R. Trueman, *The Rise and Triumph of the Modern Self: Cultural Amnesia, Expressive Individualism, and the Road to Sexual Revolution* (Crossway, 2020).

9. Sri Aurobindo, *The Human Cycle* (Ashram Trust, 1997), 17.

10. Antonin Artaud, *Collected Works*, Vol. 4 (John Calder, 1974), 19.

11. "Woman Jumps On Funeral Pyre Of Father, Who Died Of Covid; Hospitalised," Outlook, May 6, 2021.

12. Hindol Sengupta, "When the rich fall ill," Fortune India, April 25, 2021.

13. Manoj Joshi, "A medieval society? Instead of coping as a coherent democracy, we have had to revert to family and jati networks," *Times of India*, April 24, 2021.

14. Karishma Vaswani, "Coronavirus: The detectives racing to contain the virus in Singapore," BBC, March 19, 2020.

15. Nicholas A. Christakis, *Apollo's Arrow* (Little, Brown Spark, 2020), 113.

16. David Wallace-Wells, "How the West Lost COVID," *New York*, March 15, 2021.

17. Li Yuan, "In a Topsy-Turvy Pandemic World, China Offers Its Version of Freedom," *New York Times*, January 4, 2021.

18. Peter Hessler, "How China Controlled the Coronavirus," *New Yorker*, August 10, 2020.

19. "Wuhan buses hit the road after two-month lockdown," Xinhua, March 25, 2020.

20. Jane Cai and Holly Chik, "How China's army of food delivery drivers helped keep country going during outbreak," *South China Morning Post*, April 7, 2020.

21. Fang Fang, *Wuhan Diary: Dispatches from a Quarantined City* (HarperCollins, 2020), 38.

22. Iris Deng, Tracy Qu and Che Pan, "The coronavirus has

forever altered technology's role in education and work in China," Inkstone, March 26, 2020.

23. *Simmel on Culture: Selected Writings*, ed. David Patrick Frisby and Mike Featherstone (Sage, 1997), 73.

24. Aurobindo, *The Human Cycle*, 21.

25. Oriol Güell, "Hemos pecado de exceso de confianza. Nadie pensaba en esto," *El País*, March 14, 2020.

26. "'We must not stop living': French mayor defends Smurf rally that drew thousands amid coronavirus fears," *Washington Post*, March 11, 2020.

27. Mattia Ferraresi, "A coronavirus cautionary tale from Italy: Don't do what we did," *Boston Globe*, March 13, 2020.

28. Kelsey D. Atherton, "We're on the Brink of Cyberpunk," *Slate*, April 8, 2020.

29. Ray Kurzweil, "AI-Powered Biotech Can Help Deploy a Vaccine in Record Time," *Wired*, May 19, 2020.

30. Dennis Burton and Eric Topol, "Variant-proof vaccines— invest now for the next pandemic," *Nature*, February 8, 2021.

31. James Hamblin, "One Vaccine to Rule Them All," *Atlantic*, April 26, 2021.

32. Christakis, *Apollo's Arrow*, 116–17.

33. Aurobindo, *The Human Cycle*, 40–41.

2. STAR WARS

1. Koris Schake, *Safe Passage, The Transition from British to American Hegemony* (Harvard University Press, 2017).

2. Robert Gilpin, *War and Change in World Politics* (Cambridge University Press, 1981), 198.

3. Kinling Lo and Kristin Huang, "Xi Jinping says 'time and momentum on China's side' as he sets out Communist Party vision," *South China Morning Post*, January 12, 2021.

4. Stella Yifan Xie, Eun-Young Jeong and Mike Cherney, "China's economy Powers Ahead While the Rest of the World Reels," *Wall Street Journal*, January 13, 2021.

5. 王毅：民主不是可口可乐，全世界一个味道, Sina, April 24, 2021.

6. Finbarr Bermingham and Sidney Leng, "China trade: exports surge to record levels, as coronavirus lockdowns return to the West," *South China Morning Post*, December 7, 2020.

7. Jonathan Cheng, "China Exports Boom to Record Year, While Covid-19 Ravages Global Economy," *Wall Street Journal*, January 14, 2021.

8. Enda Curran, "China's Export Engine in High Gear Floods the World With Stuff," Bloomberg, January 14, 2021.

9. He Huifeng and Finbarr Bermingham, "China's makers of lockdown goods eyeing next windfall as coronavirus shutdowns return to the West," *South China Morning Post*, November 11, 2020.

10. Shuji Nakayama and Hiona Shiraiwa, "Freight rates spike as Asian cargo ships jam US West Coast ports," *Nikkei Asia*, April 3, 2021.

11. Ana Swanson, "With Americans Stuck at Home, Trade With China Roars Back," *New York Times*, December 14, 2020.

12. "Containers in short supply as Chinese exports surge," Xinhua, December 15, 2020.

13. Lisa Baertlein, "Busiest U.S. seaport, buried in imports, plucks out toys to load Santa's sleigh," Reuters, December 16, 2020.

14. Brad Setser, "China's Surplus is Rising Rapidly. So is the U.S. Deficit. The IMF cannot Turn a Blind Eye," Council on Foreign Relations, October 20, 2020.
15. U.S. Department of the Treasury, "Macroeconomic and Foreign Exchange Policies of Major Trading Partners of the United States", Report to Congress, April 2021.
16. Lawrence Summers, "The Biden stimulus is admirably ambitious. But it brings some big risks, too," *Washington Post*, February 4, 2021.
17. Tom Hancock and Jinshan Hong, "A $60 billion U.S. Stimulus Windfall Is Heading China's Way," Bloomberg, March 24, 2021.
18. Edward Luce, "Biden's big fiscal gamble on America's future," *Financial Times*, April 8, 2021.
19. James Politi, "Yellen defends higher taxes as necessary to contain deficit," *Financial Times*, May 2, 2021.
20. Bruno Maçães, *The Dawn of Eurasia* (Allen Lane, 2018).
21. Nicholas Lardy and Tianlei Huang, "China's Financial Opening Accelerates," Peterson Institute for International Economics, Policy Brief 20–17, December 2020.
22. He Huifeng, "China's factories must be 'armed with automation', as coronavirus gives boost to machines in manufacturing," *South China Morning Post*, January 10, 2021.
23. Reshma Kapadia, "The Renminbi Will Gain Wider Use Globally, Gavekal's CEO Says," *Barron's*, December 5, 2021.
24. Henry M. Paulson Jr., "China Wants to Be the World's Banker," *Wall Street Journal*, December 9, 2020.
25. Enda Curran and Bei Hu, "Ray Dalio Is Bullish on Chinese Bonds on Growth and Yield Bet," Bloomberg, November 2, 2020.

26. Louis Gave, "The 10 Important Changes Of The Past Year," Gavekal, December 15, 2020.

27. Kevin Warsh, "Beijing's Bid for Financial Supremacy," *Wall Street Journal*, January 4, 2021.

28. "Holistic Review of the March Market Turmoil," Financial Stability Board, November 17, 2020.

29. Jamil Anderlini, "Xi Jinping faces China's Chernobyl moment," *Financial Times*, February 10, 2020.

30. Anthony Galloway, "Coronavirus gives Australia a chance in Indo-Pacific: security expert," *Sydney Morning Herald*, March 2, 2020.

31. 抗击新冠肺炎疫情的中国行动, www.gov.cn, June 7, 2020 (last accessed May 21, 2021).

32. "China calls its 'heroic' handling of Covid-19 proof of its wisdom," *Economist*, October 17, 2020.

33. 李毅答《新京报》熊志, 中华复兴网, November 24, 2020.

34. Jake Sullivan and Kurt Campbell, "Competition without Catastrophe: How America Can Both Challenge and coexist with China," *Foreign Affairs*, September/October 2019.

35. John McKinnon and Alex Leary, "TikTok Sale to Oracle, Walmart Is Shelved as Biden Reviews Security," *Wall Street Journal*, February 10, 2021.

36. Hal Brands and Jake Sullivan, "China Has Two Paths to Global Domination," *Foreign Policy*, May 22, 2020.

37. H. R. McMaster and Gary D. Cohn, "America First Doesn't Mean America Alone," *Wall Street Journal*, May 30, 2017.

38. Didi Tang, "China threat to halt US antibiotics supply," *The Times*, March 11, 2019.

39. "The Biden Plan to Rebuild U.S. Supply Chains and Ensure the U.S. Does Not Face Future Shortages of Critical Equipment," www.joebiden.com (last accessed May 21, 2021).

40. Aime Williams and Claire Bushey, "White House scrambles to address global chip shortage," *Financial Times*, February 11, 2021.

41. Cheng Ting-Fang and Lauly Li, "Intel challenges Taiwan's TSMC in chip foundry business," *Nikkei Asia*, March 24, 2021.

42. U.S. Department of Defense, "Industrial Capabilities: Report to Congress," January 2021.

43. Noam Scheiber, "The Biden Team Wants to Transform the Economy. Really," *New York Times*, February 11, 2021.

44. Anna Swanson, "In Washington, 'Free Trade' Is No Longer Gospel," *New York Times*, March 17, 2021.

45. Jonas Parello-Plesner, "An 'Economic Article 5' to Counter China," *Wall Street Journal*, February 11, 2021.

46. Chris Nuttall, "Foxconn calls time on Chinese era," *Financial Times*, August 12, 2020.

47. 中共中央政治局常务委员会召开会议 中共中央总书记习近平主持会议, www.people.cn, May 15, 2020 (last accessed May 21, 2021).

48. 国家中长期经济社会发展战略若干重大问题, 求是, November 1, 2020.

49. 从当前经济形势看我国"双循环"新发展格局, Xinhua, July 9, 2020.

50. Bruno Maçães, *Belt and Road: A Chinese World Order* (Hurst, 2018).

51. Valentina Pop, Sha Hua and Daniel Michaels, "From

Lightbulbs to 5G, China Battles West for Control of Vital Technology Standards," *Wall Street Journal*, February 8, 2021.

52. Werner von Siemens, *Personal Recollections* (Asher, 1893), 390.

53. P Prem Kumar, "Coronavirus slows China-funded $100bn city in Malaysia," *Nikkei Asia*, July 7, 2020.

54. Karen Yeung, "Severe backlog in Europe-bound trains at Chinese border, as coronavirus increases rail freight volume," *South China Morning Post*, July 6, 2020.

55. John McBeth, "China building Indonesia into an EV powerhouse," *Asia Times*, February 4, 2021.

56. Adnan Aamir, "China moves for more control over Belt and Road in Pakistan," *Nikkei Asia*, February 11, 2021.

57. Isaac Chotiner, "An Indian Political Theorist on the Triumph of Narendra Modi's Hindu Nationalism," *New Yorker*, May 24, 2019.

58. Samuel Huntington, *The Clash of Civilizations and the Remaking of World Order* (Simon & Schuster, 2007 [1997]), 66.

59. Joseph Campbell, *The Hero with a Thousand Faces* (Princeton University Press, 2004), 47.

3. ESCAPE VELOCITY

1. Henry Mance, "What will we take from this year?," *Financial Times*, December 18, 2020.

2. Jacob Siegel, "Our deathwish," *Tablet*, June 12, 2020.

3. "Virus lays bare the frailty of the social contract," *Financial Times*, April 3, 2020.

4. Shawn Donnan, "A Nation's Economy Divided: Breadlines vs. Bread Makers," *Bloomberg*, December 29, 2020.

5. Nick Bilton, "'All These Rich People Can't Stop Themselves': The Luxe Quarantine Lives of Silicon Valley's Elite," *Vanity Fair*, August 13, 2020.

6. "There Aren't Enough Ventilators to Cope With the Coronavirus," *New York Times*, March 18, 2020.

7. Andreas Malm, *Corona, Climate, Chronic Emergency: War Communism in the Twenty-First Century* (Verso, 2020), 62.

8. Ilan Ben Zion, "Israel's data-for-vaccines deal with Pfizer raises privacy concerns," *Times of Israel*, January 18, 2021.

9. James Politi, "Biden unveils $2tn infrastructure plan and big corporate tax rise," *Financial Times*, March 31, 2021.

10. Eric Levitz, "Biden Doesn't Need to Be FDR or LBJ to Change America," *New York*, March 27, 2021.

11. James Crabtree, "Coronavirus: Asia embraces big government to battle recession," *Nikkei Asia*, November 25, 2020.

12. "Coronavirus Will Change the World Permanently. Here's How," *Politico*, March 19, 2020.

13. Neil Irwin, "The Coronavirus Pandemic Is Showing Us How Capitalism Is Amazing, and Inadequate," *New York Times*, November 14, 2020.

14. "Riding high in a workers' world," *Economist*, April 10, 2021.

15. Pol Antràs, "De-Globalisation? Global Value Chains in the Post-COVID-19 Age," National Bureau of Economic Research, Working Paper 28115, November 2020.

16. "Risk, resilience, and rebalancing in global value chains," McKinsey, Report, August 6, 2020.

17. David Pilling, Harry Dempsey, Peter Campbell and Kana

Inagaki, "New Suez crisis: a global economy creaking under the strain," *Financial Times*, March 26, 2021.

18. Joe Miller, David Keohane and Kana Inagaki, "Car manufacturing hit by global semiconductor shortage," *Financial Times*, January 8, 2021.

19. Debby Wu, "Missing Chips Snarl Car Production at Factories Worldwide," Bloomberg, January 11, 2021.

20. Harry Dempsey and Benjamin Parkin, "India's Covid surge rocks global shipping industry," *Financial Times*, May 6, 2021.

21. Willy C. Shih, "Global Supply Chains in a Post-Pandemic World", *Harvard Business Review* (September/October 2020).

22. Song Jung-a, "Samsung shifts some smartphone production to Vietnam due to coronavirus," *Financial Times*, March 6, 2020.

23. Peter Williamson, "De-Globalisation and Decoupling: Post-COVID-19 Myths versus Realities," *Management and Organization Review* 17(1) (February 2021), 29–34.

24. Gillian Tett, "Reports of globalisation's death are greatly exaggerated," *Financial Times*, December 3, 2020.

25. Nancy Keates, "Covid-19 Ushers in a New Era of Full-Time Travel," *Wall Street Journal*, December 7, 2020.

26. Tyler Cowen, *The Great Stagnation* (Penguin, 2011).

27. Robert Gordon, "Is U.S. Economic Growth Over? Faltering Innovation Confronts the Six Headwinds," National Bureau of Economic Research, Working Paper 18315, August 2012.

28. Alan Ohnsman, "Peter Thiel Says Covid Marks 21st Century's True Start. SPAC Boom, Surging EV Stocks Are A Sign," *Forbes*, December 3, 2020.

29. Elie Dolgin, "Unlocking the potential of vaccines built on messenger RNA," *Nature*, October 16, 2019.

30. "AlphaFold: a solution to a 50-year-old grand challenge in biology," www.deepmind.com, November 30, 2020 (last accessed May 21, 2021).

31. Eli Dourado, "Notes on technology in the 2020s," www.elidourado.com, December 31, 2020 (last accessed May 21, 2021).

32. Caleb Watney, "Cracks in the great stagnation," Agglomerations, November 23, 2020.

33. "Walmart will use fully driverless trucks to make deliveries in 2021," The Verge, December 15, 2020.

34. Henry Fountain, "Compact Nuclear Fusion Reactor Is 'Very Likely to Work,' Studies Suggest," *New York Times*, September 29, 2020.

35. David Roberts, "Geothermal energy is poised for a big breakout," Vox, October 21, 2020.

36. Charlotte Ryan and Will Mathis, "Airbus Bets on Hydrogen to Deliver Zero-Emission Jets," Bloomberg, December 4, 2020.

37. Andrew Jones, "China to launch a pair of spacecraft towards the edge of the solar system," SpaceNews, April 16, 2021.

38. Zephyr Penoyre and Emily Sandford, "The Spaceline: a practical space elevator alternative achievable with current technology," arXiv:1908.09339, submitted August 2019.

39. Justina Lee, "Top Quant Analyst Rebukes the Industry: 'I'm No Longer a Quant,'" Bloomberg, October 5, 2020.

40. Katia Porzecanski and Hema Parmar, "Renaissance, Two

Sigma Drop as Quants Navigate Chaos," Bloomberg, November 17, 2020.

41. Rana Foroohar, "Bitcoin's rise reflects America's decline," *Financial Times*, February 14, 2021.

42. Bradley Keoun, "Bitcoin Prices in 2020: Here's What Happened," Coindesk, December 30, 2020.

4. A NEW PLANET

1. William F. Ruddiman, "The Anthropogenic Greenhouse Era Began Thousands of years Ago," *Climatic Change* 61 (2003), 261–93.

2. Simon Lewis and Mark Maslin, *The Human Planet: How We Created the Anthropocene* (Penguin, 2018), 13.

3. John Gray, *The Soul of the Marionette* (Penguin, 2015).

4. Peter Brannen, "The Terrifying Warning Lurking in the Earth's Ancient Rock Record," *Atlantic*, March 2021.

5. Walther Rathenau, the German industrialist and statesman, called industrialization a "dumb process of nature."

6. Adam Tooze, "We are living through the first economic crisis of the Anthropocene," *Guardian*, May 7, 2020.

7. Monica H. Green, "The Four Black Deaths," *American Historical Review* 125(5) (December 2020), 1601–31.

8. Nicholas Wade, "The origin of COVID: Did people or nature open Pandora's box at Wuhan?" *Bulletin of the Atomic Scientists*, May 5, 2021.

9. Craig Welch, "Half of All Species Are on the Move—And We're Feeling It," *National Geographic*, April 27, 2017.

10. Emilie Alirol et al., "Urbanisation and infectious diseases in a globalised world," *The Lancet Infectious Diseases* 11(2) (February 2011), 131–41.

11. Harald Brüssow, "Europe, the bull and the Minotaur: the biological legacy of a Neolithic love story," *Environmental Microbiology* 11(11) (November 2009), 2778–88, 2779.

12. Christophe Bonneuil and Jean-Baptiste Fressoz, *The Shock of the Anthropocene: The Earth, History and Us* (Verso, 2017).

13. Tyler Cowen, "The Politics of Covid Just Got Even More Hellish," Bloomberg, January 5, 2021.

14. Alexandre Koyré, *From the Closed World to the Infinite Universe* (Harper, 1958), 84.

15. Frank Herbert, *Dune* (Berkley Publishing Co., 1977), 277.

16. Amitav Ghosh, *The Great Derangement* (University of Chicago Press, 2017), 7.

17. James Carse, *Finite and Infinite Games* (Simon & Schuster, 2011).

18. Arnold Gehlen, *Man in the Age of Technology* (Columbia University Press, 1980), 2.

19. Matthew Karnitschnig, "Europe's leaders rated on their coronavirus response," *Politico Europe*, October 17, 2020.

20. "Top Official: Israel in 'final stages' of COVID, showing world an exit strategy," *Times of Israel*, January 15, 2021.

21. Ernesto Londoño and Letícia Casado, "Brazil Needs Vaccines. China Is Benefiting." *New York Times*, March 15, 2021.

22. Yaroslav Trofimov and Eric Bellman, "In Covid-19 Diplomacy, India Emerges as a Vaccine Superpower," *Wall Street Journal*, February 12, 2021.

23. "The EU should stop ignoring the vaccine race to try and win it," *Economist*, January 23, 2021.

24. "No more vaccine exports until you fulfill your contracts, EU tells AstraZeneca," Reuters, March 25, 2021.

25. Rowland Manthorpe, "COVID-19: rejected contracts and a Hollywood movie—how UK struck deal to guarantee vaccine supply," Sky News, February 1, 2021.

26. "EU's vaccine failure is because it didn't 'shoot for the stars,' Macron says," Reuters, March 24, 2021.

27. Simon Parkin, *Death by Video Game: Tales of Obsession from the Virtual Frontline* (Serpent's Tail, 2015).

28. Uri Friedman, "The Pandemic Is Revealing a New Form of National Power," *Atlantic*, November 15, 2020.

29. Karl Haushofer, "Politische Geographie und Geopolitik", in *Freie Wege vergleichender Erdkunde. Erich von Drygalski zum 60. Geburtstag gewidmet von seinen Schülern* (München, Leipzig, 1925), S. 87–103.

30. Christian Yates, "Why all the world's coronavirus would fit in a can of cola," BBC, February 10, 2021.

31. Andreas Malm, *Corona, Climate, Chronic Emergency: War Communism in the Twenty-First Century* (Verso, 2020), 14.

32. "Global COVID-19 death toll more than double official estimates—IHME," Reuters, May 6, 2021.

33. David Wallace-Wells, *The Uninhabitable Earth: Life After Warming* (Crown, 2019), 51.

34. Michaël Aklin and Matto Mildenberger, "Prisoners of the Wrong Dilemma: Why Distributive Conflict, Not Collective Action, Characterizes the Politics of Climate Change," *Global Environmental Politics* 20(4) (November 2020), 4–27.

35. John Dizard, "Decarbonisation goals require huge com-

mitment to critical metals," *Financial Times*, December 24, 2020.

36. Michael Peel and Henry Sanderson, "EU sounds alarm on critical raw materials shortages," *Financial Times*, August 31, 2020.

37. David Wallace-Wells, "The war on climate denial has been won. And that's not the only good news," *New York*, January 19, 2021.

38. Pierre Charbonnier, "For an ecological realpolitik," *e-flux Journal* 114, December 2020.

39. Jane Cai, "Tracing China's climate change journey from denial to decarbonisation," *South China Morning Post*, April 20, 2021.

40. Janka Oertel, Jennifer Tollmann and Byford Tsang, "Climate Superpowers: How the EU and China Can Compete and Cooperate for a Green Future," European Council of Foreign Relations, Policy Brief, December 2020.

41. Scott Moore, "Why China's New Climate Commitments Matter for U.S. National Security," Lawfare, October 13, 2020.

42. Leslie Hook and Henry Sanderson, "How the race for renewable energy is reshaping global politics," *Financial Times*, February 4, 2021.

43. Ilaria Mazzocco, "Beijing Lines Up the Pieces for Peaking Emissions by 2030," Macropolo, April 7, 2021.

44. William Gibson, *The Peripheral* (Penguin, 2014).

45. Shannon Osaka, "After a century of growth, have carbon emissions reached their peak?" Grist, December 29, 2020.

46. "After steep drop in early 2020, global carbon dioxide

emissions have rebounded strongly," IEA, Press Release, March 2, 2021.

47. A. Gettelman, R. Lamboll, C. G. Bardeen, P. M. Forster and D. Watson-Parris, "Climate impacts of COVID-19 induced emission changes," *Geophysical Research Letters* 48 (2021).

48. Richard Betts, "Met Office: Atmospheric CO2 now hitting 50% higher than pre-industrial levels," Carbon Brief, March 16, 2021.

49. David Wallace-Wells, "Global Warming Is Melting Our Sense of Time," *New York*, June 27, 2020.